The Beatles
Unseen Archives

The Beatles
Unseen Archives

Photographs by the

𝕯𝖆𝖎𝖑𝖞 𝕸𝖆𝖎𝖑

Compiled by

Tim Hill and Marie Clayton

p

This is a Parragon Book
This edition published in 2002

Parragon
Queen Street House
4 Queen Street
Bath, BA1 1HE, UK

All photographs ©Associated Newspapers Ltd
Text ©Parragon

Produced by Hazar Publishing Ltd

Designed by John Dunne
Origination by Croxons PrePress

A catalogue record for this book is available from the
British Library.
ISBN 0 75258 368 9

Printed in China

Contents

Introduction

Four lads who shook the world

Revisiting past glories and pleasures can often be an unrewarding experience. The glitter of any golden age tarnishes all too easily; the treasures of youth can appear dated and embarrassing just a few short years later. Those who were swept along with the tide of Osmondmania or Rollermania may have fond memories of the time, but it's doubtful whether the tartan cut-offs or 'Puppy Love' get much of an airing today.

The Beatles had more than their share of hype and hysteria; all the trappings and excesses of pop superstardom were there. They didn't have to play a note to send audiences into raptures and once the audience was in raptures, the notes were hardly worth playing. The deafening screams swamped the puny Vox amplifiers in those early days and the four of them sometimes gave in and stopped performing. The fans appeared not to realize - or to care.

But after Beatle jackets and haircuts were outgrown, after the flimflam and froth were stripped away, there remained the unique melding of four individual talents. They produced a canon of work with a timeless quality, music for all succeeding generations to discover and enthuse over. It is said that Brian Wilson, the creative genius behind the Beach Boys, abandoned the project he was working on after hearing *Sgt Pepper* for the first time. He didn't see the point of going on now that the definitive album had been made.

The Beatles not only dominated the musical landscape during their years together, but influenced it immeasurably after they went their separate ways. At the site of the original Cavern Club in Mathew Street there is a legend which puts it succinctly: 'Four lads who shook the world'. *The Beatles: Unseen Archives* recaptures that seismic phenomenon.

Acknowledgements

The Photographs from this book were taken by Associated Newspapers' photographers and are from the archives of the *Daily Mail*.

Many of these fabulous photographs, taken by some of the world's leading professionals, are from negatives never previously printed. The photographers' work has been carefully archived by the very dedicated staff in the Picture Library resulting in one of the last great remaining photographic treasures chronicling The Beatles.

The pleasure this book will give to the fans of the greatest rock band of the twentieth century is a tribute to the continued diligence and hard work of the team. Many thanks to David Sheppard and the present staff and all those who have held this important responsibility before them, including:

Brian Jackson	Oscar Courtney
Alan Pinnock	Andrew Young
John Bater	Rachel Swanston
Derek Johnson	David Lavington
David Stanley	Robert Sanders
Tom McElroy	Andrew Eva
Leslie Adler	Bill Beasley
Tony Fordham	Charles Whitbread
Steve Cooper	Philip Lambourne
Derek Drew	Carol Hooper
Steve Murray	Chris Nelthorpe
Raymond Archer	Denis Hoy
Terry Aylward	Bob Dignum
	Paul Howard

Thanks also to Christine Hoy, John Dunne, Cliff Salter, Lee Sherwood, Paul Rossiter, Richard Betts, Keith Lock, Ian Withers Alan Hatherly and Alison Gauntlett.

Particular thanks to Steve Torrington without whom this book would not have been possible.

Finally, thanks to the late Sir David English who was so inspirational and who would have enjoyed seeing the finished book.

The Beatles
Unseen Archives

Chapter One

The Early Years

Ticket To Ride

Everyone knows that The Beatles came from Liverpool, but their distinctive sound and their talent for reaching an audience came not from the bars and clubs of their home town, but from their exhaustive stints far away in Hamburg. Until they went to Germany, the band was a constantly changing collection of part-time musicians, with a hard core of three members: John Lennon and Paul McCartney, both on rhythm guitar, and George Harrison on lead. They played anywhere they could – private parties, youth clubs, working men's clubs – not only changing the line-up regularly, but also experimenting with different names for the group.

Until 1960 the band had no permanent drummer or a bass guitarist, so when John's art-college friend Stu Sutcliffe won £60 in an art contest he was promptly persuaded to invest in a bass guitar even though he couldn't play. The band had earlier met local club-owner Allan Williams, who began to book them into gigs round Liverpool and even got them an audition which led to a short tour round Scotland, backing singer Johnny Gentle. In the middle of 1960, Williams was looking for another group to send to Hamburg and the only one available to go was... The Beatles. He offered them the booking, on condition they found themselves a competent drummer. One of their regular venues was the Casbah Club and Pete Best, son of the owner, had his own drum kit. He was quickly recruited into

The Beatles, and off they went to Germany.

In Hamburg the five Beatles – John, Paul, George, Stu and Pete – had to play ridiculously long hours every night in the same venue in front of demanding customers. They not only became a much more tightly-knit group, they also had to develop a dynamic stage presence and a louder, more raunchy playing style to satisfy the often drunken audience. Another major influence on their style was photographer Astrid Kirchherr, who took atmospheric pictures of them around the city and cut Stu's hair into the famous mop-top later adopted by John, Paul and George.

In addition, the band expanded their repertoire and came to know the songs so well that they were able to develop and perfect the sound that later took the world by storm. The line-up was also soon on its way to the final four: Stu left the group to live with Astrid, leaving Paul to take over bass guitar, and they became friendly with Ringo Starr, who was in Hamburg with Rory Storm and the Hurricanes. After The Beatles returned to Liverpool at the end of 1960, they were booked to appear at Litherland Town Hall. Their new sound and extrovert stage show exploded on to a stunned British audience, and things were never the same again.

It was not long before word of this dynamic new group spread round Liverpool and came to the ears of Brian Epstein, a local businessman and record-store owner. He came to see them at the Cavern Club one lunchtime and promptly decided he wanted to manage them – even though he had never managed a band before. He immediately took the boys in hand, making sure they turned up to bookings on time, tidying up their stage show and getting rid of their 'greasy rocker' image by banning their leather gear and putting them all into suits. He also started looking for a recording contract and finally got the group an audition at Decca – who turned them down. Brian was incensed, but he didn't give up and in May 1962 George Martin of Parlophone finally agreed to take them on.

One problem still remained – Martin was not keen on Pete Best's drumming style. This could perhaps have been resolved, but George, Paul and John took it as an opportunity to get rid of Pete, who they felt didn't fit in, and invite Ringo to join them instead. Pete had been with them for nearly two years but none of them was prepared to tell him to his face, so they left the task to Brian. It was all handled very badly.

Ringo joined The Beatles in mid-August, so he had just over two weeks of playing with them before they recorded their first single, 'Love Me Do'/'PS I Love You'. It was released in October and managed to reach No 17 in the charts – if rumors are to be believed, mainly because Brian Epstein bought up 10,000 copies.

Although The Beatles now had one record out and were due to appear on their first London TV program, they were still almost completely unknown outside Merseyside – but not for long. Throughout 1963 they worked a punishing schedule, which included four national British concert tours, two Scottish tours, one short Swedish tour and numerous one-night shows. They made two LPs, three EPs and four singles, a multitude of TV and radio recordings, and attended many photographic sessions and Press interviews. No reasonable request for their time was refused by Brian Epstein. Their second single was released early in the year and, after a rapid climb, hit the number-one spot towards the end of February. At the time The Beatles were on a tour supporting Helen Shapiro, but gradually they became the major attraction. For the following tour they were supposed to be supporting two American stars, Tommy Roe and Chris Montez, but soon took over as top of the bill.

In August, The Beatles gave their last-ever show at the Cavern; it could no longer contain the vast crowds of Beatle fans and anyway they had outgrown their local following. The BBC were not slow to pick up on the group's growing popularity: after many radio show appearances, the boys were offered their own radio series, *Pop Go The Beatles*, which ran over four weekly programs. The Beatles also appeared on BBC television so many times that cynics began to dub it the 'Beatles Broadcasting Corporation'. They already had their own

monthly magazine, *The Beatles Book*, and an official fan club, which had grown from a few thousand to 80,000 paid-up members by the end of 1963.

Even early in the year, Beatle-inspired mania had begun to break out locally around Britain, although it was only in October that the national newspapers finally began to pick up on the story. A live appearance by The Beatles on the network TV show, *Val Parnell's Sunday Night at the London Palladium*, which led to crowds of hysterical fans gathering outside the normally staid theater in the center of London, finally caught their attention. The next day the papers were full of stories about fans rioting and breaking through a police cordon when the boys tried to leave the theater. A couple of weeks later The Beatles returned to Heathrow airport from a short tour of Sweden and were stunned by the thousands of fans who had gathered in the rain to welcome them back, along with a full complement of reporters and photographers.

Since the national fame of The Beatles had arrived so suddenly, they soon found themselves having to fulfil bookings made months previously for fees that were ludicrously low in comparison to what they could now command. Brian Epstein did occasionally try to buy them out of some of these dates if he thought that the proposed venue would no longer be safe, but otherwise he never went back on a signed contract. A much more serious problem was the increasingly manic behavior of the fans, which had now become dangerous both to themselves and the group. Girls cried, screamed, tried to throw themselves at their favorite Beatle or grab pieces of clothing or snippets of hair, or simply fainted. Even in the small town of Carlisle, 600 fans queued for up to 36 hours in freezing weather for the box office to open. When it did, the surge forward resulted in nine people being taken to hospital. At larger venues the casualties sometimes ran into hundreds. It was a major logistical exercise to get the band to and from the venue in safety, and once inside they had to stay cooped up in their dressing-rooms, prisoners of their own fame. When thay actually made it onto the stage, they had to dodge around to avoid being hit by the gifts and packets of jelly babies thrown by fans.

For The Beatles themselves the growing Beatlemania was at first flattering, but quickly went beyond a joke and began to be a cause of some resentment. Concert tours were already a mind-numbing routine of arriving in a town, being smuggled into the venue, performing a show, being hustled out into a van for a high-speed getaway to a nearby hotel, and then holing up overnight until it was time to go through it all again the next day. They had to wear elaborate disguises to go out in public, their homes and those of their families were under constant siege from fans, articles were stolen from their dressing-rooms and the piercing screams throughout concerts meant that no one – not even The Beatles themselves – could hear the music.

But they had already changed the British music scene for ever. Before this, popular musical trends had invariably started in America and major stars were American, while London had a stranglehold on the British scene. Now Liverpool suddenly became fashionable and Merseyside took over the pop charts. Gerry and the Pacemakers, Cilla Black, the Searchers, Billy J. Kramer and the Dakotas all owed their success to The Beatles - and most of them were also managed by Brian Epstein.

Previous page: The sweet smile of success. At the end of 1962, Brian Epstein had been buying up copies of 'Love Me Do' by the bucketload to ensure chart success; within a few short months, advance copies of Beatles records were selling in their hundreds of thousands.

Below: The Beatles are very thinly disguised as policemen in order to get past the huge crowds gathering for a concert outside the Birmingham Hippodrome.

The Early Years: Chronology

1934

19 September   Brian Epstein is born in Liverpool

1939

10 September   Cynthia Powell is born in Blackpool

1940

23 June   Stuart Sutcliffe is born in Edinburgh, Scotland

7 July   Ringo Starr is born at the Royal Liverpool Children's Hospital

9 October   John Lennon is born at the Oxford Street Maternity Hospital, in Liverpool

1941

24 January   Randolph Peter Best is born in Madras, India

1942

18 June   Paul McCartney is born at Walton Hospital, Liverpool

1943

25 February   George Harrison is born at home at 12 Arnold Grove, Wavertree, Liverpool

1957

March   John forms The Black Jacks skiffle group with Pete Shotton, which is later renamed The Quarry Men

9 June   The Quarry Men audition for Carroll Levis' *TV Star Search* at Liverpool's Empire Theatre, but fail to qualify

6 July   Paul meets John for the first time, when he sees The Quarry Men play at St Peter's Church garden fete in Liverpool

20 July   Paul is invited to join The Quarry Men

7 August   The Quarry Men perform at the Cavern Club in Liverpool for the first time

18 October   Paul's debut performance with The Quarry Men, at the New Clubmore Hall, Liverpool. He played lead guitar, but made a mess of his solo and was demoted to rhythm

1958

6 February   George meets The Quarry Men and is later invited to join them because of his growing skill as a guitarist, although he is younger than the others

15 July   Julia, John's mother, is killed by a speeding car when crossing the road after leaving his Aunt Mimi's house

1959

25 March   Ringo joins Rory Storm and the Hurricanes, at that time Merseyside's top band

29 August   The Quarry Men play at the opening night of the Casbah Club, owned by Pete Best's mother. The group consists of John, Paul, George and Ken Brown. They still have no drummer

10 October   Ken Brown quits The Quarry Men

15 November   As Johnny and the Moondogs, John, Paul and George make the final audition for Carroll Levis' *TV Star Search* at Liverpool's Empire Theatre

1960

January   Stuart Sutcliffe, a friend of John at the Art College, joins The Quarry Men as bass player

May   The Quarry Men become The Beatals

10 May   The Beatals become The Silver Beetles and audition as a backing group for Billy Fury, but instead are booked to tour Scotland as backing for singer Johnny Gentle

20-28 May   The Silver Beetles tour Scotland. The group have also changed their own names: 'Long John' Lennon, Paul Ramon (McCartney), Carl (George) Harrison and Stu de Stael (Stuart Sutcliffe). Tommy Moore (his real name) plays the drums

June   The Silver Beetles become The Beatles before reverting to The Silver Beetles

July   The Silver Beetles become The Silver Beatles

12 August   Pete Best joins The Silver Beatles as drummer

16 August   The group finally becomes The Beatles and sets off for Hamburg

17 Aug-3 Oct   The Beatles play at the Indra Club on Hamburg's Grosse Freiheit

4 Oct-30 Nov   The Beatles play at the Kaiserkeller Club

15 October   John, Paul, George and Ringo record together for the first time, with bassist Walter Eymond of Rory Storm and the Hurricanes, at Akustic Studio, Hamburg

10 November   John leaves Hamburg

21 November   George is deported from West Germany for being under-age for nightclub work after midnight

29 November   Paul and Pete are thrown into jail for apparently setting fire to their living quarters at the Bambi cinema

30 November   Paul and Pete are released from jail but deported. Stu stays in Germany with his girlfriend, Astrid Kirchherr

27 December   The Beatles perform at the Litherland Town Hall in Liverpool, inciting the first scenes of Beatlemania

1961

9 February   The Beatles perform for the first time at the Cavern Club, in a lunchtime session

21 March	The Beatles perform for the first time in an evening session at the Cavern
27 Mar-2 Jul	The Beatles make their second trip to Hamburg, to play at the Top Ten Club on the Reeperbahn
22-23 June	The Beatles play in a professional recording studio for the first time, backing singer Tony Sheridan and performing a couple of numbers without him for producer Bert Kaempfert
9 November	Brian Epstein visits the Cavern Club at lunchtime to see The Beatles performing

3 December	The Beatles attend their first business meeting with Brian Epstein, at his record store
6 December	Brian Epstein offers to manage the group and John accepts on their behalf
9 December	The Beatles play their first concert down south at the Palais Ballroom, Aldershot, but it is not advertised so only 18 people turn up
13 December	A&R man Mike Smith of Decca Records comes to see The Beatles play at the Cavern Club

Below: George sends another autograph-hunter away happy. The first Harrison song to feature on a Beatles record is 'Don't Bother Me' on the new LP, *With The Beatles*. He would later describe it as a 'crappy' song, instantly forgettable. It would be two years before he would contribute another song to The Beatles' canon, on the *Help!* album.

1962

1 January	The Beatles audition for Mike Smith and Dick Rowe at Decca, recording 15 songs
4 January	The Beatles top a popularity poll in local music paper, *Mersey Beat*
24 January	The Beatles sign a management contract with Brian Epstein, although Epstein himself does not sign
February	Decca Records turn down The Beatles
13 February	Brian Epstein meets George Martin, EMI Records' head of A&R, and plays him the recording of The Beatles' failed Decca audition
7 March	The Beatles make their radio debut, recording at Manchester's Playhouse Theatre for the BBC's *Teenager's Turn (Here We Go)*, which is transmitted the following day
10 April	Stuart Sutcliffe dies of a brain hemorrhage aged 21
13 Apr–31 May	The Beatles make their third trip to Hamburg, to perform at the new Star-Club on Grosse Freiheit
9 May	Brian Epstein meets George Martin again, and The Beatles are offered a recording contract, depending on an audition/recording session scheduled for 6 June
6 June	The Beatles perform the audition/recording session at EMI studios in Abbey Road and are formally offered a record deal
15 August	Ringo is invited to join The Beatles and accepts
16 August	Pete Best is fired as The Beatles' drummer
18 August	Ringo makes his debut as a Beatle, at Hulme Hall in Port Sunlight, Birkenhead
22 August	The Beatles are filmed at the Cavern by Granada Television, but the footage is shelved until they become famous the following year
23 August	John marries Cynthia Powell at Liverpool's Mount Pleasant Register Office
4 September	The Beatles return to Abbey Road for their first formal recording session with Ringo
1 October	Brian Epstein finally signs the management contract with The Beatles
5 October	Their first single, 'Love Me Do'/'PS I Love You', is released in the UK and reaches No 17 in the charts
17 October	The Beatles make their TV debut with a live appearance on Granada Television's *People And Places*, which was broadcast to the north and north-west
1-14 Nov	The Beatles' fourth season in Hamburg, a two-week booking to play at the Star-Club
18-31 Dec	The Beatles' fifth and final stint in Hamburg, again playing at the Star-Club

1963

2-6 January	The Beatles travel around Scotland for their first concert tour
11 January	Their second single, 'Please Please Me'/'Ask Me Why', is released in the UK (25 February in the US)
19 January	The Beatles make their national TV debut on *Thank Your Lucky Stars*, playing 'Please Please Me'
2 February	The Beatles begin their first proper package tour of Britain, supporting Helen Shapiro
2 February	The first London newspaper coverage of The Beatles appears in the *Evening Standard*, a general feature by Maureen Cleave
11 February	The Beatles record ten new tracks for their first album, *Please Please Me*, in just under ten hours
19 February	The 'Please Please Me' single tops both the *New Musical Express* and *Disc* magazine charts, although it only reaches No 2 on the BBC chart
9 March	The Beatles embark on their second British concert tour, supporting Chris Montez and Tommy Roe
22 March	Their first LP, *Please Please Me*, is released in the UK and tops the British charts
5 April	The Beatles receive their first silver disk, for selling 250,000 copies of their single, 'Please Please Me'
8 April	John and Cynthia have a son, John Charles Julian
11 April	The Beatles' third single, 'From Me To You'/'Thank You Girl', is released in the UK (27 May in the US). It is the first of eleven consecutive singles to top the British charts through to 1966
18 April	Paul meets young actress Jane Asher after a BBC radio concert broadcast live from the Royal Albert Hall
18 May	The Beatles start their third British tour
4 June	A BBC radio series, *Pop Go The Beatles*, is launched
21 June	'Beatle in brawl' headline appears in the *Daily Mirror*, reporting that John got drunk and beat up Cavern DJ Bob Wooler at Paul's 21st birthday party in Liverpool on 18 April
12 July	The EP *Twist And Shout* is released in the UK
16 July	The Beatles record 17 songs for three separate episodes of their show, *Pop Go The Beatles*
22 July	The LP *Introducing The Beatles* is first released in the US only. It is re-released in the US on 27 January 1964
1 August	Publication of the first issue of *The Beatles Book*, a monthly magazine about the group
3 August	The Beatles play for the last time at the Cavern Club
13 August	The EP *Twist And Shout* sells 250,000 copies and becomes the first of its genre to qualify for silver status
23 August	The single 'She Loves You'/'I'll get You' is released in the UK (16 September in the US)
3 September	The Beatles record a further 18 songs for another three separate episodes of *Pop Go The Beatles*
6 September	The EP *The Beatles' Hits* is released in the UK
10 September	The Beatles receive the award for Top Vocal Group of the Year at the Variety Club Awards lunch at the Savoy hotel
15 September	The Beatles share the bill with the Rolling Stones at the annual *Great Pop Prom* at the Royal Albert Hall, London
5 October	A three-day tour of Scotland begins at the Concert Hall, Glasgow
13 October	A live appearance by The Beatles on the network TV show, *Val Parnell's Sunday Night at the London Palladium*, causes a sensation across Britain
23 October	The Beatles fly to Sweden for their first proper foreign concert tour
31 October	Thousands of fans gather at London Airport to greet The Beatles on their return from Sweden

1 November	First night of The Beatles' Autumn Tour of Britain, in Cheltenham, Gloucestershire	16 November	Clark's Grammar School in Guildford, Surrey becomes the first school to send boys home for sporting a Beatles haircut
1 November	The EP *The Beatles (No 1)* is released in the UK	22 November	The LP *With The Beatles* is released in the UK
2 November	The *Daily Mirror* coins the term 'Beatlemania', when reviewing the Cheltenham show	29 November	The single 'I Want To Hold Your Hand'/'This Boy' is released in the UK. In the US the B side is 'I Saw Her Standing There' and the single is released on 26 December
4 November	The Beatles appear at the *Royal Variety Performance*, where John asks the audience to rattle their jewellery	24 December	*The Beatles' Christmas Show* begins at the Astoria Cinema, Finsbury Park, London. It runs for 16 nights
6 November	The footage filmed by Granada Television at the Cavern Club in 1962 is finally shown on *Scene At 6.30*		
9 November	George signs a five-year music publishing contract with Northern Songs		
9 November	After their show in East Ham, The Beatles go to a party in London given by millionaire John Bloom		

Below: George dances the night away at a party given by millionaire John Bloom.

'I haven't seen anything like this...'

Paul and John's prodigious songwriting talent comes to the fore in 1963. They begin the year by stubbornly refusing George Martin's suggestion to record 'How Do You Do It?' as a follow-up to 'Love Me Do', insisting on writing their own material. (Gerry and the Pacemakers were subsequently offered the song and took it to No 1 in the charts.)

Below: After their triumphant appearance on *Sunday Night at the London Palladium*, the boys try to wrong-foot fans by leaving via the front exit, rather than the stage door. Ringo, John, Paul and road manager Neil Aspinall show concern as they emerge to find no waiting vehicle.

Opposite above: The getaway car has been parked some way up Argyll Street, where police hoped it would look less conspicuous. By the time Paul and Ringo reach it, the fans are in hot pursuit. 'I haven't seen anything like this since Johnny Ray appeared in 1955,' said George Cooper, the theatre's stage doorman.

Opposite below: The Beatles in an off-duty moment at a TV studio in Birmingham. The hectic touring commitments continue, but Epstein recognizes the impact of television exposure. Record sales quadruple on the day following the *Palladium* appearance, and Epstein is already targeting the top-rated *Ed Sullivan Show* as a bridgehead for The Beatles' assault on America.

'Rattle your jewellery'

Opposite and right: Thousands of fans gather at London Airport as the Beatles return from a five-day trip to Sweden. They create a bigger security headache than Prime Minister Sir Alec Douglas-Home, who happens to be passing through the airport at the same time. By pure chance, one witness to the chaotic scenes is the very person Epstein wants to do business with - Ed Sullivan himself.

Below: Rehearsing on 4 November for the *Royal Variety Performance* at the Prince of Wales Theatre. The nineteen-act bill includes Max Bygraves, Harry Secombe, Tommy Steele, Marlene Dietrich and Pinky and Perky. The Beatles are seventh on stage but, predictably, steal the show with a set comprising 'From Me To You', 'She Loves You', 'Till There Was You' and 'Twist and Shout'. However, the evening is probably best remembered for the celebrated 'ad lib' with which John introduces the final number: 'Will those in the cheaper seats clap your hands; the rest of you can just rattle your jewellery.'

Mop-tops...

Below: Close-up mop-top. Beatles wigs are just one example of the vast merchandising industry which accompanies Beatlemania. Epstein fails to realize the full potential of this market. He enters into an agreement in which 90% of merchandising profits go to a company set up to handle all such matters. One of the earliest deals was with a clothing company which paid $100,000 for the right to produce Beatle T-shirts. Epstein thought this sum ludicrous, until he discovered that the company recouped this outlay in just three days. It would be 1967 before this disastrous arrangement was ended, by which time it was estimated that The Beatles had lost $100 million.

Right and opposite: Ringo dances with music publisher's wife Mrs Lou Levy at a Mayfair party given by millionaire John Bloom. 68-year-old porter Arthur Dyer proves to be slightly out of touch with popular culture by refusing to let The Beatles in at first, believing them to be gatecrashers instead of VIP guests.

A quiet night out

Paul's hopes for a quiet evening out with Jane Asher are dashed as he becomes the centre of attention at a West End theatre.

Opposite: There is no better endorsement for a garment than to have a Beatle wear it. Here, as the boys arrive for a concert in Huddersfield, Ringo sports a corduroy coat. The ailing corduroy industry is said to have The Beatles to thank for a huge growth in sales during this period.

Flying high in the charts

Swapping a drumstick for a joystick. Ringo tries his hand at the controls of the Viking aircraft taking some of the biggest names in pop from Liverpool to London. Brian Epstein had chartered the plane at a cost of £400 to give Ringo and other members of his Mersey Sound stable a break from *The Beatles' Christmas Show*, at the Astoria, Finsbury Park.

The Beatles had cause to be pleased with themselves in December '63. Advance sales of their new single, 'I Want To Hold Your Hand', hit the one million mark, while orders for the new LP *With The Beatles* stand at 250,000 - a record for an album.

Chapter Two

1964

A Hard Day's Night

If 1963 was the year that Beatlemania hit Britain, 1964 was the year when The Beatles conquered the rest of the world. Their first stop was Paris, but the shows here were not a success. The Beatles themselves were not satisfied with how things were organized, nor with their playing at the first concert, and one of the amplifiers cut out so many times that sabotage was suspected. The audience at the second concert was mainly Parisiennes in evening dress, rather than young rock fans, so the band received a cool reception. This was the concert the French Press attended, so reviews were similarly cool. These problems did not affect them long, however, as news suddenly came by telegram that 'I Want To Hold Your Hand' had shot from No 43 to No 1 in the music charts in America.

Soon all the group's records were climbing up the American charts - just days before they were due to visit New York to appear on *The Ed Sullivan Show* and to give concerts at the Washington Coliseum and Carnegie Hall. Their reception at John F. Kennedy Airport was wildly enthusiastic, as America succumbed to The Beatles in a typically whole-hearted fashion. The viewing figures for *The Ed Sullivan Show* smashed the existing world record for the largest-ever audience for an entertainment show, and during The Beatles' ten-minute spot there were no hub caps reported stolen in New York - which was also a first!

As well as visiting New York and Washington The Beatles also spent a few days in Miami, where they not only appeared live on *The Ed Sullivan Show* again and taped a third performance to be shown later, but also managed a few days of rest and relaxation. Wherever the boys went the now-familiar scenes of pandemonium unfolded yet again as American fans went crazy.

After their brief visit to America, the group returned home to begin their first film, *A Hard Day's Night*, at Twickenham. The storyline was based on incidents from their own lives, with all four Beatles playing their parts with great confidence. Meanwhile, Beatlemania was taking hold across the rest of the world. By the beginning of April, Beatles singles occupied the top five positions in the American *Billboard* chart and the top six positions in the singles charts in Sydney.

After four weeks off in May, the longest rest The Beatles had managed for some considerable time, they were ready to begin their first world tour, starting in Denmark. The day before their departure Ringo collapsed during a photo-shoot and was rushed to hospital suffering from tonsillitis and pharyngitis. Although George felt that they couldn't go without Ringo and wanted to cancel the tour, Brian Epstein and George Martin persuaded him that this was impossible. Instead, Jimmy Nicol, a very experienced but relatively unknown session drummer, became the temporary replacement for Ringo. Just hours after Ringo's collapse, Nicol went to EMI's

Abbey Road studios to rehearse six numbers with the world's greatest supergroup and the following day he was on his way to Denmark.

Beatlemania now followed the band wherever they appeared, not just at the concert venues in Denmark, The Netherlands, Hong Kong, Australia and New Zealand but also wherever the plane touched down for refuelling. Day or night, in even the remotest of places, crowds of screaming fans appeared out of nowhere to try and catch a glimpse of their idols. Ringo rejoined The Beatles in Australia, just in time for their first concert in Melbourne. Their reception across the country was even more manic than it had been in America: in Melbourne, an estimated 250,000 people gathered outside their hotel and in Adelaide the crowd was over 300,000 – many more than had ever turned out to see them in either Britain or even in America.

After a few bookings in Britain and another short tour to Sweden, The Beatles then set off on their first full American tour. It consisted of 32 shows in 24 cities within 34 days - which would perhaps have been reasonable in Britain, but was far too much in a land the size of America. John, Paul, George and Ringo spent almost the entire time travelling and, except for journeying to and from concert venues and airports, they were unable to leave their hotels. They saw very little of any of the places they visited, only the crowds of rampaging fans everywhere they went.

Kansas City was not originally included in the tour, but Charles O. Finlay, the millionaire president of the Kansas City Athletics baseball team, was determined to get The Beatles for his city and offered the unprecedented sum of $150,000 for them to appear for one night at Kansas City Stadium. After their visit, the 16 sheets and eight pillowcases from their hotel beds were sold to two Chicago businessmen for $750. The linen was left unlaundered, cut into three-inch squares, mounted on a card with a legal affidavit and sold at $10 a time. The towels used by The Beatles to mop their faces after the concert were also cut up and sold.

When The Beatles returned to Britain from America, to the usual hysterical scenes at London Airport, the Prime Minister, Sir Alec Douglas-Home, called them 'our best exports' and 'a useful contribution to the balance of payments'.

Below: Seeing double - The Beatles and their wax-work equivalents at Madame Tussaud's.
Previous page: Paul, George, Ringo and John enjoy some winter sunshine in Miami at the end of their first trip to the USA.

1964: Chronology

3 January	A clip of The Beatles is shown on *The Jack Paar Show* in the US
15 January	The Beatles perform in Versailles, France, before starting a two-week season at the Olympia Theatre in Paris
20 January	The LP *Meet The Beatles* is released in the US
25 January	In America's *Cashbox* magazine, 'I Want To Hold Your Hand' jumps 43 places to top the singles chart
30 January	The single 'Please Please Me' is re-released in the US only, with 'From Me To You' as the B side
7 February	The EP *All My Loving* is released in the UK
7 February	The Beatles arrive at Kennedy Airport in New York
9 February	The Beatles make a landmark television appearance on *The Ed Sullivan Show*, watched by 73 million viewers
11 February	The Beatles' US debut concert, at the Washington Coliseum
12 February	Two more concerts, at Carnegie Hall back in New York
12 February	A hastily-made documentary about The Beatles' US visit is shown on UK television
13 February	The Beatles fly from New York to Miami, to do their second *Ed Sullivan Show* and have a few days off to relax
16 February	The second *Ed Sullivan Show* featuring The Beatles is watched by 70 million viewers
22 February	The Beatles return to England
2 March	A single, 'Twist And Shout'/'There's A Place', is released in the US only
2 March	The Beatles begin shooting their first film, *A Hard Day's Night*
10 March	Ringo does the pub sequences for the film in Twickenham
16 March	The single 'Can't Buy Me Love'/'You Can't Do That' is released in the US (20 March in the UK)
19 March	The Beatles collect their Variety Club of Great Britain 1963 Showbusiness Personalities of the Year award
23 March	The Duke of Edinburgh presents The Beatles with Carl-Alan awards
23 March	John's first book, *In His Own Write*, is published and the first print run quickly sells out
23 March	A single, 'Do You Want to Know a Secret'/'Thank You Girl', is released in the US
3 April	The Beatles hold the top six positions in a singles chart in Sydney, Australia
4 April	Beatles singles are also in the top five positions in America's *Billboard* chart
10 April	An LP, *The Beatles' Second Album*, is released in the US
23 April	John attends a Foyle's literary luncheon in his honour
27 April	A single, 'Love Me Do'/'PS I Love You', is released in the US
29 April	The Beatles arrive in Scotland for two concerts
6 May	ITV screen their own TV special, *Around The Beatles*
21 May	A single, 'Sie Liebt Dich'/'I'll Get You', is released in the US
May	Madame Tussaud's unveil their models of The Beatles
3 June	Ringo collapses with tonsillitis and pharyngitis just prior to The Beatles' first world tour. He is temporarily replaced by session drummer Jimmy Nicol
4 June	The world tour begins with a concert in Copenhagen, Denmark
11 June	The Beatles arrive in Sydney, Australia
15 June	Ringo rejoins The Beatles in Australia and performs with them from Melbourne onwards
19 June	The EP *Long Tall Sally* is released in the UK
26 June	The LP *A Hard Day's Night* is released in the US (10 July in the UK)
6 July	*A Hard Day's Night* has its royal world charity première at the London Pavilion cinema
10 July	The single, 'A Hard Day's Night'/'Things We Said Today', is released in the UK. In the US the B side is 'I Should Have Known Better' and the single is released on 13 July
12 July	A concert at the Hippodrome, Brighton, is the first of five summer concerts at British seaside resorts
20 July	Two singles, 'I'll Cry Instead'/'I'm Happy Just to Dance With You' and 'And I Love Her'/'If I Fell' are released in the US
20 July	An LP, *Something New*, is released in the US
23 July	The Beatles appear in a charity show, *The Night of A Hundred Stars*, at the London Palladium
18 August	The Beatles leave London Airport for their first US concert tour
24 August	A single, 'Matchbox'/'Slow Down', is released in the US
17 September	The Beatles are paid $150,000 to play Kansas City Municipal Stadium on their day off, earning around £1,785 per minute
9 October	Another UK tour begins at the Gaumont Cinema, Bradford. The Beatles are joined by Motown star, Mary Wells
6 November	The EP *Extracts From The Film A Hard Day's Night* is released in the UK
6 November	The EP *Extracts From The Album A Hard Day's Night* is released in the UK
8 November	The first concert in Liverpool for nearly a year is held at the Liverpool Empire
23 November	An LP, *The Beatles' Story*, is released in the US
23 November	The single, 'I Feel Fine'/'She's A Woman', is released in the US (27 November in the UK)
1 December	Ringo holds a Press conference about his tonsils
4 December	The LP *Beatles For Sale* is released in the UK
15 December	A different LP, *Beatles '65*, is released in the US
24 December	*Another Beatles Christmas Show* begins at the Odeon, Hammersmith and runs until 16 January 1965

She loves you...

Below: George takes advantage of a brief respite in the relentless schedule to return home to Liverpool.

Harold and Louise Harrison help him pack for the America trip. Some of George's gear goes into his 'BEA-TLES' travel bag, the airline company's latest merchandising gimmick. In return for displaying the bags prominently, the boys were given free flights between London and Paris.

Below right: He gets a kiss from proud mum and number one fan Louise, who encouraged his early efforts with the guitar and attended a lot of the early gigs.

Opposite: John and George on their way to France, where lukewarm audiences get the year off to an inauspicious start.

Right: Singer Sylvie Vartan tries out one of Ringo's cameras during the Beatles' 18-day residency at the Olympia Theatre, Paris. Both Vartan and American singer Trini Lopez go down better than The Beatles with the French audiences, but the boys are buoyed by the news that they have become the first British group to top the US charts with 'I Want to Hold Your Hand'.

The Beatles Are Coming!

The Lennons at London Airport, preparing to fly out to New York. The fact that one of the Beatles was married with a child had only recently been uncovered by prying Fleet Street reporters.

Opposite above: 'The Beatles Are Coming!' That was the message on hoardings and on the airwaves right across the USA.

Opposite below: Apart from the two *Ed Sullivan Show* appearances, The Beatles give just three performances during their 15-day America trip: one concert at Washington Coliseum, and two shows at Carnegie Hall.

Washington

The Washington venue had the boys on a revolving stage. This had unfortunate consequences, for it not only afforded the whole audience a better view, but it also made the group a target to a lot more people. It had been reported that George had a particular weakness for jelly babies; this fondness proved painful in Washington, for the stage was peppered from all angles with these mini-missiles.

Drowned out

The Beatles were doing their best to belt out their material, but their Vox amplifiers were nowhere near up to the task in a venue full of screaming teenagers.

Look this way boys...

More photo calls on their flying visit.

The two Carnegie Hall concerts are hugely successful and massively over-subscribed, and as a result there was a last-minute attempt to organize a show at Madison Square Garden - at double the Carnegie Hall fee - but this proved impossible.

Live across America...

The Beatles play pass-the-phone at their New York Press conference. From their suite at the Plaza Hotel the boys innocently take some real calls, which turn out to be from DJs. Many of these go out on the air, and when Epstein discovers what is going on, he is furious at the small fortune's worth of interview material that they have given away for free.

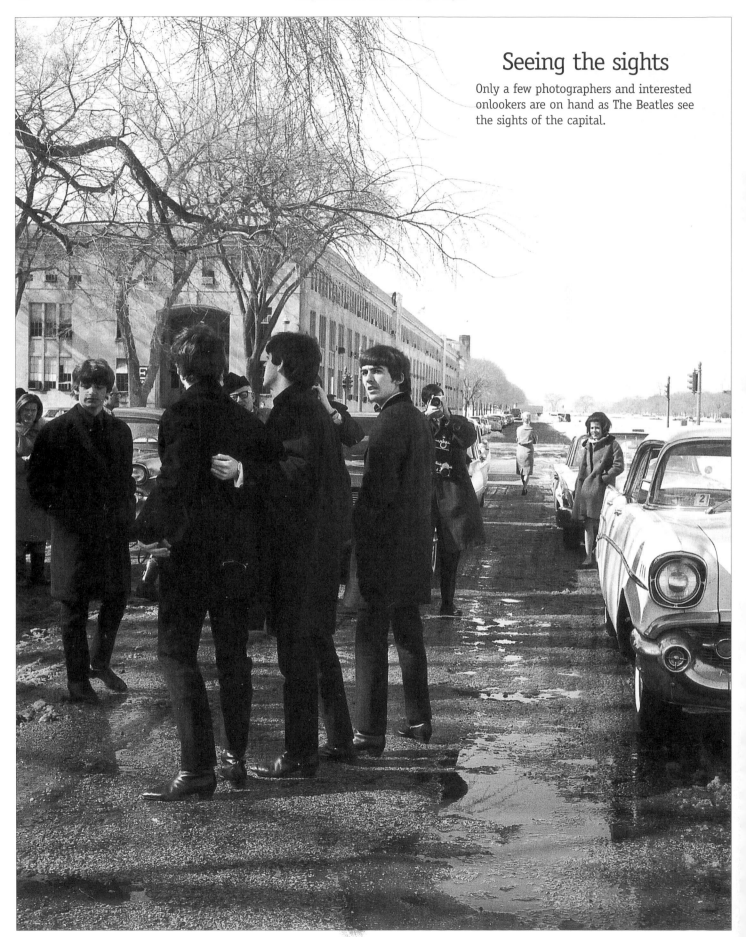

Seeing the sights

Only a few photographers and interested onlookers are on hand as The Beatles see the sights of the capital.

'Not quite hopeless'

Reviews of *The Ed Sullivan Show* are mixed, including this from the New York Journal-American: 'Sartorially they're silly, tonsorially they're wildly sloppy, musically they're not quite hopeless'. The estimated 73 million audience begs to differ.

Epstein had targeted the top-rated show to get exposure for the group, after 'Love Me Do', 'Please Please Me' and 'She Loves You' had all failed to make an impression. The *Sullivan Show* wanted the Beatles as a novelty support act; Epstein wanted a top-of-the-bill slot. The deal ultimately thrashed out - headlining two shows on consecutive weeks for a total fee of just $7000. Epstein used the show as a huge loss-leader in order to break into the US market.

Opposite: All aboard in Miami.

Miami

A far cry from ferrying across the Mersey. The boys go cruising off the Miami coast aboard the luxury yacht *Southern Trail*. Their second appearance on *The Ed Sullivan Show*, on 16 February, is another triumph, with the audience again hitting the 70 million mark.

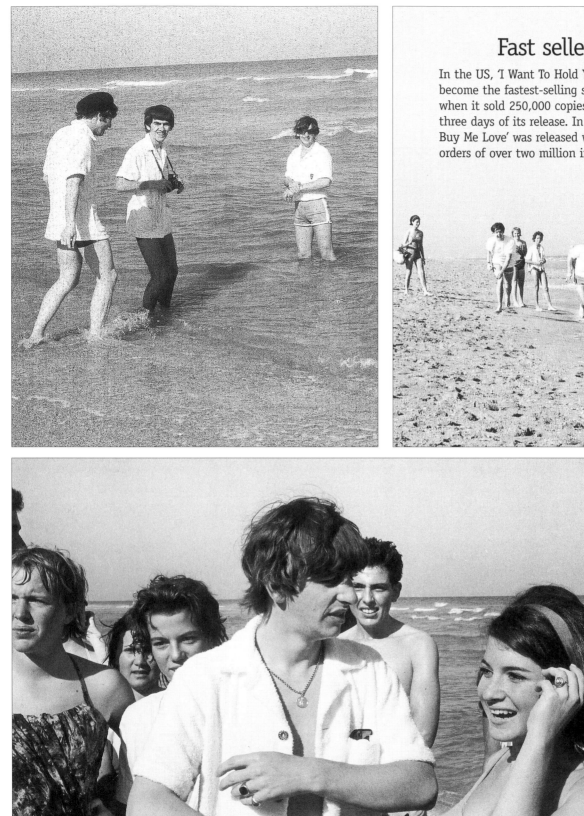

Fast sellers...

In the US, 'I Want To Hold Your Hand' had become the fastest-selling single to date when it sold 250,000 copies within the first three days of its release. In March, 'Can't Buy Me Love' was released with advance orders of over two million in the US alone.

The Greatest

The Beatles come up against Cassius Clay, who is in Miami for his 25 February world title showdown with Sonny Liston. Clay declares that he's still the greatest, but The Beatles are the prettiest. Both parties come to world prominence in 1964 and go on to dominate their respective fields for the rest of the decade.

The Beatles returned to England on 22 February. A 36-minute documentary programme on their US visit was shown on British television while they were away.

Above: Waiting for 'The Greatest', Cassius Clay.

Below and opposite: Making a publicity appearance in the US under the watchful eye of Brian Epstein.

George's jam butties...

Opposite below: With filming for *A Hard Day's Night* just under way, the boys are invited to dine at Brasenose College, Oxford. John recollects his Chaucer studies at school; George trades his smoked salmon for jam butties. (*l to r:* Paul, George, student Michael Lloyd, principal Sir Noel Hall, tutor Mr David Stockton, Ringo, John).

Opposite above right: Ringo with Sir Noel Hall.

This page: Around the time of George's 21st birthday, The Beatles taped an appearance for the variety show *Big Night Out*.

A Hard Day's Night

Right: These four lucky girls not only appear in The Beatles' film as fans, but also get the job of running their combs through the most famous hair in the world. No wonder it's smiles all round from (*l to r*) Pattie Boyd, Tina Williams, Pru Bury and Susan Whiteman.

Below: Paul relaxes at the piano during a break from filming at Twickenham Studios.

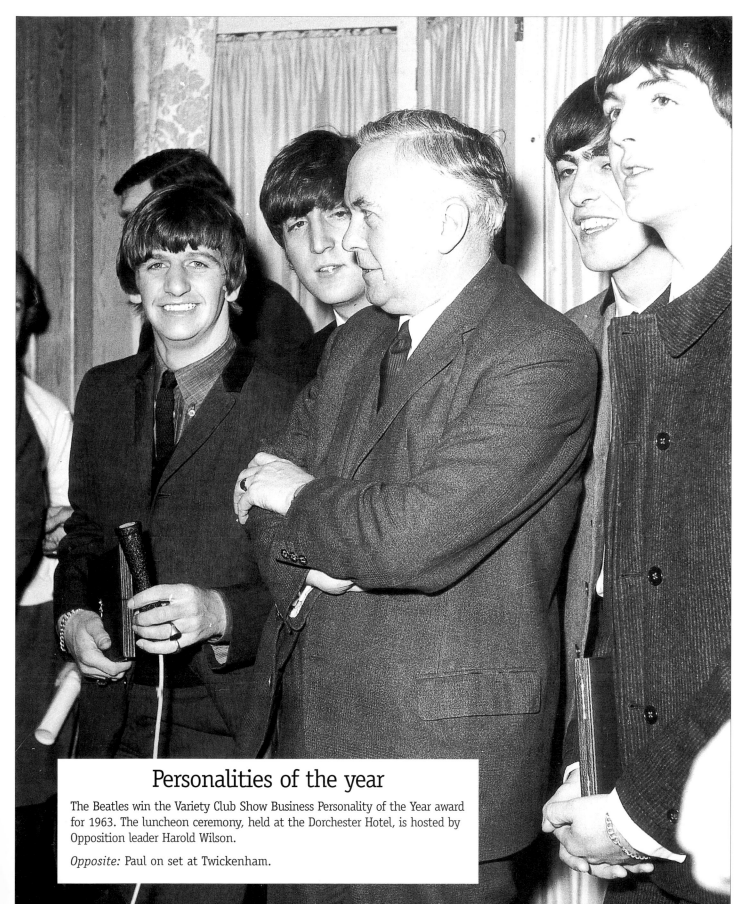

Personalities of the year

The Beatles win the Variety Club Show Business Personality of the Year award for 1963. The luncheon ceremony, held at the Dorchester Hotel, is hosted by Opposition leader Harold Wilson.

Opposite: Paul on set at Twickenham.

'The Nation is Proud'

Labour Party Leader Harold Wilson presented the awards during the Variety Club Luncheon at the Dorchester Hotel on 19 March: 'I will refrain from making political capital out of The Beatles...we are all proud of the creation of a new musical idiom in the world of communications.'

Wilson takes a sideswipe at Prime Minister Sir Alec Douglas-Home's recent comments regarding The Beatles as a valuable export commodity for Britain.

Thumbs up and a speech from George as
the group of the year celebrate their award.

John enjoys a nice cup of tea with Mary Wilson as the celebrations continue at the Variety Club awards luncheon.

Ready, Steady, Go!

March 20 is Beatles night on television. The group perform live on ATV's *Ready, Steady, Go!*, with the Variety Club awards ceremony broadcast later the same evening.

Opposite above: The boys put their feet up during a break in filming at the Scala Theatre, while John takes the opportunity to publicize his book. Also pictured is producer Walter Shenson, who had negotiated a three-film deal with Brian Epstein the previous autumn. Shenson, working on behalf of United Artists, was hoping to exploit a loophole in The Beatles' EMI recording contract, which did not cover movie soundtracks. This meant that even if the movie bombed, there would be lucrative album sales to make up for it.

Opposite below: The Duke of Edinburgh presents the Carl-Alan awards at the Empire Ballroom, Leicester Square. The Beatles win two awards: Best Group of 1963, and Best Vocal Record, for 'She Loves You'.

I'm happy just to dance with you...

MP Bessie Braddock gets a close-up view of what the Prime Minister calls 'our best exports'.

Opposite: Paul celebrates their latest honour with a Havana cigar. There's little time for resting on laurels, however. The following day sees the release of 'Can't Buy Me Love', which goes straight to No 1 on both sides of the Atlantic. Hardly surprising, as advance orders had been a world-record three million.

Ringo has a strum and a smoke when not required on set at the Scala Theatre, where the performance scenes for *A Hard Day's Night* were shot. Filming was hindered by a dispute over the unpaid extras used for the audience, which was only resolved when the 350 extras were given £3 15 shillings with lunch thrown in. Among their number was a callow youth who would go on to make his own mark in the world of popular music: one Phil Collins.

Opposite: Filming the nightclub scene at the exclusive Les Ambassadeurs Club, London on the 17 April. The change in title from *Beatlemania* to *A Hard Day's Night* is announced in the media.

Below: Relaxing on a train.

Twist and shout

The Beatles assembled at Les Ambassadeurs Club in the afternoon to film the nightclub scene for *A Hard Day's Night*. Ringo is dancing (to 'Twist and Shout') with Maggy London. Paul is in the background (*and opposite*) with Merrill Colebrook.

When asked to comment on the title change from *Beatlemania* to *A Hard Day's Night*, the producer said 'It means something if you don't think about it too much'.

Opposite below: John is guest of honour at a Foyle's literary luncheon on 23 April, his book *In His Own Write* having been published a month earlier. John chats with Lionel Bart but disappoints the audience by declining to make a speech.

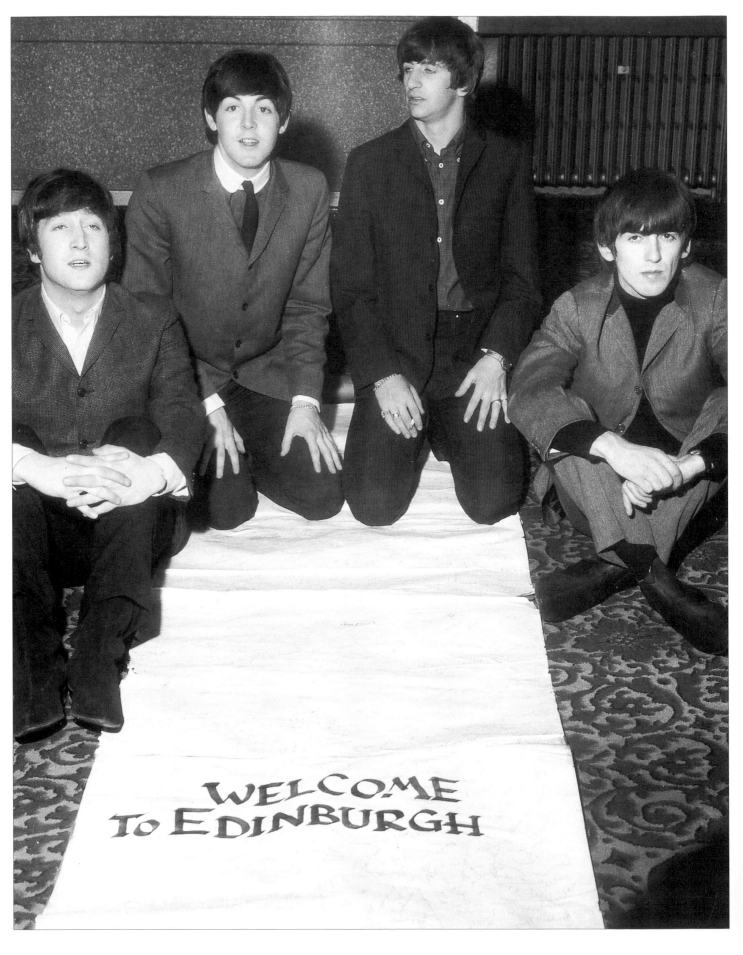

Welcome to Edinburgh

When The Beatles arrive at Turnhouse airport, Edinburgh, on 29 April for the first of two consecutive nights in Scotland, they are presented with a lucky mascot by one of their young fans, Linda McLean.

Opposite: The concerts, in Edinburgh and in Glasgow, were promoted by Albert Bonici with Brian Epstein and were both hugely successful.

In person - The Beatles

Although a few lucky fans did meet The Beatles in person, the cinema would not hold all those who had applied for tickets so there were hundreds of disappointed people outside just waiting for a glimpse of their idols. The concerts were so successful that The Beatles returned to Scotland in October, playing at Edinburgh, Dundee and Glasgow during their UK tour.

Below and opposite below: Inside, the boys sign autographs and chat to a few of the lucky ones.

PS I Love You

Fame inevitably meant meeting fans and signing endless autographs, which sometimes got The Beatles down, but in Edinburgh they seem to be enjoying all the attention from some of their younger fans.

Just a few beers...

After a disastrous charity reception at the British Embassy in Washington, where The Beatles were pushed around by junior officials and ordered to sign autographs - and where one 'distinguished' guest just walked up and snipped off a lock of Ringo's hair - the boys had refused to attend any more official functions. In Edinburgh, however, the Lord Provost sat down in the bar with them without any formality and a good time was had by all.

Opposite below: John takes a closer look at the heavy gold chain of office sported by the Lord Provost.

On stage at last. The Beatles played one concert in Edinburgh and two at the Glasgow Odeon the following night.

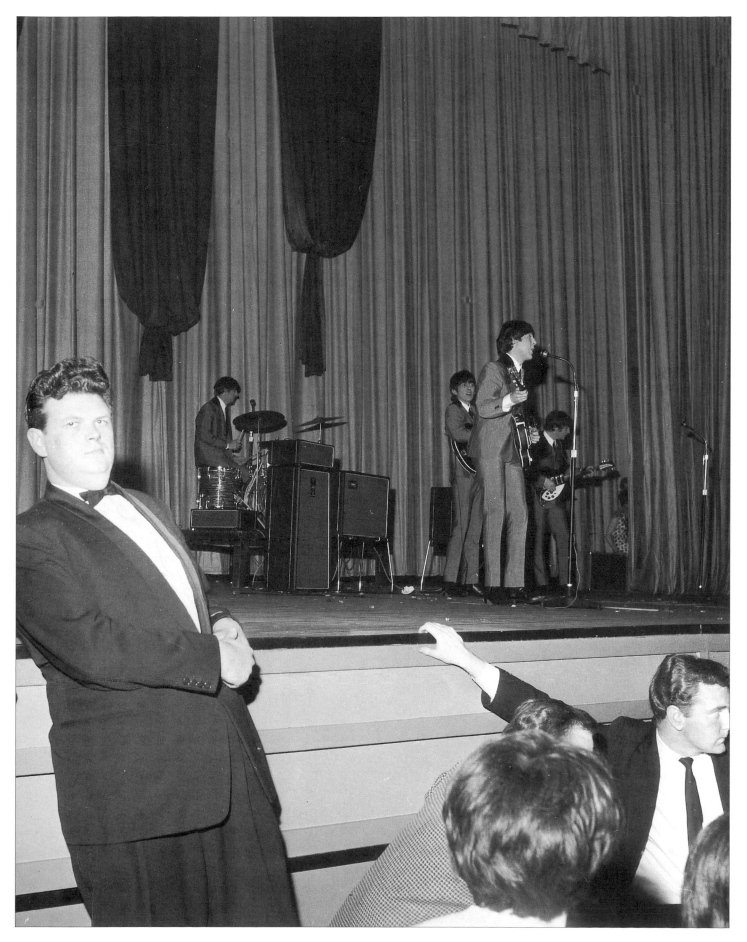

'Which way to the stage?'

Opposite and below: 'I tell you it's not that way!' The boys fool around for the cameras before they take to the stage.

While in Edinburgh, The Beatles also give an interview to BBC Scotland Radio reporter Bill Aitkenhead, which is broadcast that evening on the Scottish Home Service programme *Scottish News*.

Right: Beatlemania Scottish style.

Below right: Autograph production line.

One last photocall and the chance to meet a fan more their own age, then The Beatles are off to Glasgow.

John and Cynthia return from holiday.

Opposite and below: The boys get together at the Prince of Wales Theatre on 31 May after holidaying separately for the previous month.

Around the World

The world tour is announced. The first concert will be held in Copenhagen, Denmark and they will then take in Australia and their first concert tour of America. They also plan five summer performances at British seaside resorts.

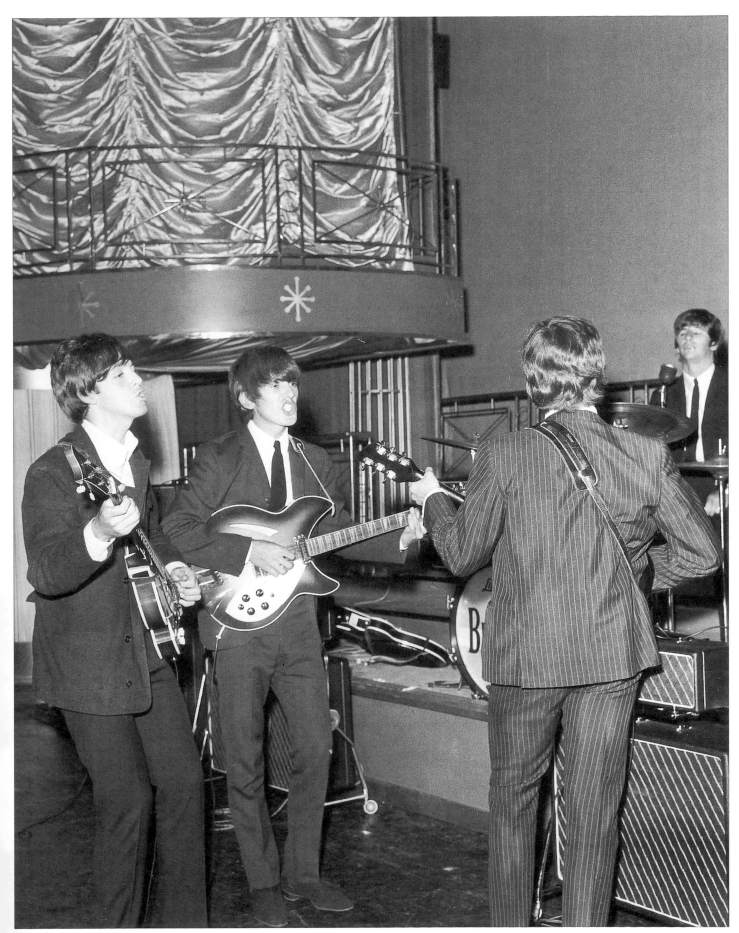

Cheers!

The Beatles drink to their forthcoming world tour at a Press conference held at the Prince of Wales Theatre in London.

Opposite bottom: Getting back in the groove; Paul preparing for two performances at the Prince of Wales Theatre.

The Beatles seemed to find themselves behind the bar for celebratory drinks on a regular basis - later in the year they toast the success of their UK tour, at the Odeon in Leeds.

Opposite below: Ringo puts on a brave face as he is admitted to University College Hospital, having collapsed at a photo-shoot earlier.

Jimmy in the nick of time...

Session drummer Jimmy Nicol gets rather more than 15 minutes of fame when he is called in as a last-minute replacement for Ringo, who is diagnosed as having tonsilitis and pharyngitis. A rehearsal at EMI Studios is hastily arranged, and Nicol gets the nod of approval.

Jimmy basks in the temporary limelight as he flies out to Denmark with John, George and Paul. He had joined Georgie Fame's Blue Flames only the week before, but this part-tour would represent the pinnacle of his musical achievement. When Ringo rejoins the group in Australia, Nicol receives £500 and a gold watch before returning to relative obscurity.

The world at their feet

Paul shows off a pair of clogs, a souvenir from the Dutch leg of the world tour.

Opposite above: The Beatles down under. The boys acknowledge their Australian fans from their 8th-floor suite in a Sydney hotel.

Opposite below: Beatle boards plane with Scarlett woman. The shot makes it look as though they are an item, but it is merely a coincidence that actress Vivien Leigh is catching the same flight for Australia as Ringo.

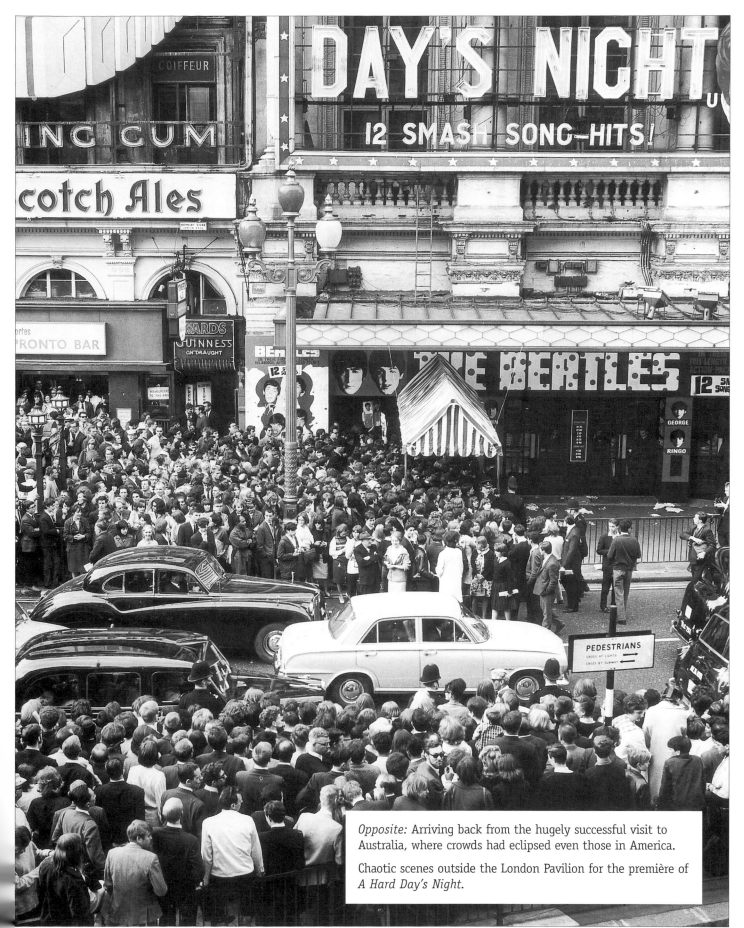

Opposite: Arriving back from the hugely successful visit to Australia, where crowds had eclipsed even those in America.

Chaotic scenes outside the London Pavilion for the première of *A Hard Day's Night*.

Liverpool lads

Opposite: Princess Margaret meets the group at the première of *A Hard Day's Night* at the London Pavilion. The LP of the same name was released a couple of weeks later and went to the top of the charts. It was the first Beatles album to feature exclusively Lennon/McCartney compositions.

Above: Liverpool honours its four favourite sons. The Beatles are given a civic reception at the Town Hall, having attended the northern première of *A Hard Day's Night*.

Right: Paul at the ABC Theatre, Blackpool.

Live in Blackpool

The Beatles appear in the live variety programme *Blackpool Night Out*, which is hosted by Mike and Bernie Winters. As well as performing some of their songs, they also appear in several comedy sketches.

Hail the conquering heroes

Having taken America by storm on their first proper US tour, a few fans think that Paul's talents would not go amiss in Parliament.

Above: Brian Epstein looks on as The Beatles wave the fans goodbye at New York's Kennedy Airport. The tour had taken in 24 cities over 34 days, with the boys playing 32 concerts. Kansas City was not part of the schedule, but a local businessman persuaded them to play a 35-minute set there for a record fee of $150,000.

Opposite: On stage in Dundee, during the Scottish leg of their UK tour.

I Feel Fine

Left: Ringo lets the world have a last look at some of the most celebrated tonsils in the world. He books into University College Hospital to have them removed.

Above: Patience with the patient. George kills time with Ringo, playing the Chinese version of the game.

Ringo leaves hospital after a week, humming the latest Beatles' No 1: 'I Feel Fine'. Just in case any ultra-determined fan has any designs on a rather exclusive, if ghoulish, piece of Beatles' memorabilia, he announces that the tonsils in question have been burned.

Opposite: Far out, man. That's The Beatles' view of Eskimo-land, which seems to them to be one of the few places they haven't visited in 1964. They deck themselves out in the appropriate gear instead, for their Christmas show at the Hammersmith Odeon.

Chapter Three

1965

Eight Days A Week

This year was really just more of the same for The Beatles. They released three singles, three EPs and two LPs and made a second film, *Help!*, a comic-strip adventure about the attempts of an obscure Middle-Eastern sect to recover a sacred sacrificial ring that a fan had sent to Ringo. This offered opportunities for location filming, so scenes in the Bahamas and Austria were written into the storyline. But the boys soon became bored during the long hours filming and turned to smoking pot to fill the time, so their concentration was not one hundred percent. Despite this, the film was shot in under three months and was released within a further two months. It did good business and was well received by the critics.

Apart from filming and recording, the group's life was still dominated by touring, with a European tour to France, Italy and Spain, another tour across America and finally a short tour around Britain. All four Beatles had begun to feel that this relentless touring with its suffocating adulation was becoming almost impossible to bear. They were now subject to death threats and the unintentional terrorization by fans was getting even more out of hand. In Houston, Texas, at 2.00 am in the morning, 5000 screaming teenagers broke through the airport barriers and a police cordon and were soon thronging round the plane, climbing on to the wings to peer through the windows and catch a glimpse of their idols. The Beatles were trapped and the pilot was unable to taxi the plane to safety as the fans were underneath it and around the wheels. The boys finally managed to escape through an emergency exit into a service truck and make their getaway.

During concerts John now quite regularly told the fans to 'Shaddup!', and they discovered that even if one of them stopped playing for a few seconds no one noticed. Their music had suffered because of the impossibility of playing well under such conditions; they had once been proud of the fact that they were a tight group of accomplished musicians, but now hardly bothered to rehearse before a tour and often ended up playing abysmally at concerts. Who could blame them when everything was totally inaudible and no one seemed to be interested in listening anyway?

As they became increasingly angered by the mayhem around them, they began to turn their attention to pleasing themselves rather than their public. It was no longer possible to develop new songs on tour as they had in the old days, so they turned more to the recording studio and to working on a progressive complexity of sound. They told Brian Epstein that they wanted to give up touring, and vetoed his suggestions of another *Royal Command Performance* and another Christmas show. He managed to talk them into one more short tour of Britain that winter, which became the last that they ever did in the UK.

This was also the year in which The Beatles received their MBEs. The announcement was received with disbelief – not only by some of the battle-scarred previous recipients who returned their awards in disgust, but also by the group themselves. They assumed they had been honoured for their services to the British export industry, rather than for playing rock music, but even so no pop artiste had been received such an award before. There was some talk initially about turning the honour down, as they all felt that it was too 'Establishment', but in the end they accepted it.

On a personal note, by now each of them was settled with a partner. John and Cynthia had been married since 1962 and had a two-year-old son, while Ringo had married Maureen at the beginning of 1965 and their first son had just been born. Paul had been seeing actress Jane Asher since 1963 and George was living with model Pattie Boyd, whom he had met on the set of *A Hard Day's Night* in 1964. Although this didn't seem to affect the group's popularity, during the height of Beatlemania the wives and girlfriends were quite often subjected to abuse and attack from hysterical fans who were convinced that they alone were destined to be with their chosen Beatle.

But Beatlemania was finally beginning to show signs of running out of steam. In 1965, for the first time, some of the concert venues were not full to capacity and far fewer fans turned up at the airports to welcome the group or wave them a fond farewell. There were still plenty of fans, but perhaps they had begun to realize that it was a waste of money to pay for seats at a concert where their heroes could be as much as 500 yards away and at which they could not hear a note of the music. But The Beatles were still amazingly popular – as Newcastle University's Professor Strang said at the time, 'You can walk down any street of the most primitive village in a country where no one speaks English and hear children chanting the words of the latest Beatles hit'.

Below: George inspects his MBE.
Previous page: The Beatles in the Bahamas filming *Help!*.

1965: Chronology

11 February   Ringo marries Mary (Maureen) Cox

12 February   The newly-married couple hold a Press conference at the beginning of their honeymoon in Hove, East Sussex

15 February   A single, 'Eight Days a Week'/'I Don't Want to Spoil the Party', is released in the US

22 February   The Beatles fly to the Bahamas to begin shooting their second film, *Help!*

13 March   After a couple of days in Britain, The Beatles fly to Austria, for more location filming

22 March   An LP, *The Early Beatles*, is released in the US

6 April   The EP *Beatles For Sale* is released in the UK

9 April   The single, 'Ticket To Ride'/'Yes It Is', is released in the UK (19 April in the US)

14 April   The communal house sequence for *Help!* is filmed in Ailsa Avenue, Twickenham

26 April   Ex-Beatle Pete Best is interviewed in the *Daily Mirror*

3-5 May   A sequence for *Help!* is filmed on Salisbury Plain

20 May   The Beatles record their last-ever music session for BBC radio

4 June   The EP *Beatles For Sale (No 2)* is released in the UK

7 June   The BBC broadcasts the last radio performance, *The Beatles (Invite You To Take A Ticket To Ride)*, which was pre-recorded on 26 May

11 June   At midnight, it is announced that The Beatles are to be awarded MBEs

14 June   An LP, *Beatles VI*, is released in the US

20 June   A short European concert tour of France, Italy and Spain starts with a concert in Paris

1 July   John's second book, *A Spaniard in the Works*, is released

19 July   The single, 'Help!'/'I'm Down', is released in the US (23 July in the UK)

29 July   *Help!* has its royal world charity première at the London Pavilion

1 August   The Beatles play live on ITV's *Blackpool Night Out*

6 August   The LP *Help!* is released in the UK (13 August in the US)

15 August   The Beatles open their second US tour with a landmark concert at New York's Shea Stadium, witnessed by a then-record audience of 55,600

27 August   The Beatles meet Elvis Presley at his Beverly Hills home on Perugia Way

13 September   Ringo and Maureen Starkey have a son, Zak

13 September   A single, 'Yesterday'/'Act Naturally', is released in the US

26 October   The Beatles receive their MBEs from the Queen in the Great Throne Room at Buckingham Palace

3 December   The Beatles start their last UK tour, playing at the Odeon Cinema, Glasgow

3 December   The single, 'We Can Work It Out'/'Day Tripper', is released in the UK (6 December in the US)

3 December   The LP *Rubber Soul* is released in the UK (6 December in the US)

6 December   The EP *The Beatles' Million Sellers* is released in the UK

17 December   ITV broadcasts *The Music of Lennon & McCartney* around Britain, except in London where it had already been transmitted the previous evening

Testing time

No more 'watching the wheels' for John as he passes his driving test at the age of 24. He receives his congratulations in the EMI Studios car park, at the wheel of George Martin's car.

Fallen idol

John parts company with one of his skis during a lesson at St Moritz. In fact, John proved quite adept on the slopes, staging the spill purely for the benefit of impatient cameramen.

Opposite: Ringo and his new bride, 18-year-old former hairdresser Maureen Cox, pose for the cameras at Hove, Sussex, where they are honeymooning at a house owned by Beatles solicitor David Jacobs. The couple had married the previous day at Caxton Hall Register Office in London - at 8.00 am to avoid the fans.

Help!

The Beatles are given a rapturous send-off at London Airport as they leave for the Bahamas, where shooting of their second film is to begin.

Eight arms to hold you...

Above: Actress Eleanor Bron is the envy of hordes of screaming teenage girls as she flies out to the Bahamas with The Beatles to co-star in *Help!*. A leading light in the satirical comedy fringe, 26-year-old Miss Bron would not have experienced anything like the mass hysteria and adulation which accompanies the Fab Four.

Right and opposite: Cooling off in the Bahamas. The project went through several working titles, including *Eight Arms To Hold You*, before director Dick Lester came up with *Help!*.

Paul and George pictured at London Airport, a couple of weeks into the 11-week shooting schedule for *Help!*.

John and Eleanor Bron on location in Ailsa Avenue, Twickenham.
Opposite and overleaf: Ringo does his best to keep warm between takes.

Off to check out the competition. Having completed filming on *Help!* a few days earlier, John flies out to the Cannes Film Festival, accompanied by Cynthia.

Paul, with Jane Asher. Speculation was rife that they were about to marry - or had done so already in secret.
Opposite: Paul on his 23rd birthday is carried aloft.

Help!

The Beatles in formal attire on the occasion of the royal charity première of *Help!* at the London Pavilion. 'We'd be much happier in jeans and T-shirts,' said George. Also pictured are Cynthia Lennon and Maureen Starr.

Drummer's boy.

Above and previous page: John, Paul, George and
Ringo acknowledge their fans as they return home
from their second US tour. A few days earlier the idols
had met their own idol - Elvis - at his Beverly Hills
home in Perugia Way, but it was not to prove an
enduring friendship.

Right and opposite: News that Maureen Starr has given
birth to a boy brings the press out in droves to Queen
Charlotte's Hospital, Hammersmith. 'He's about that
big,' (opposite above left) the proud father reveals.
Ringo is more specific about the baby's weight - 8lb -
and announces that the new arrival will be called Zak.

The Beatles, MBE

Even though news of the award had been in the public domain since 12 June, the controversy surrounding the decision remained undiminished. The honour had been conferred at the personal recommendation of Prime Minister Harold Wilson, a self-confessed Beatles fan whose constituency was Huyton, Liverpool. But many agreed with critic Bernard Levin, who was incensed that such an honour should be awarded to four men whose music he regarded as 'ephemeral rubbish'. Some returned their own medals in protest.

Opposite below: Brian Epstein now proudly presents...The Beatles, MBE. Unlike The Beatles themselves, Epstein was unequivocal in his delight at the award. Investiture protocol meant that the four could have taken two guests each to the ceremony, but they decided to meet the Queen as a group, and only their manager was invited.

The perfect cook

George has married the perfect cook. That's his mother's opinion anyway. When asked about her cooking Pattie said 'I do enjoy cooking and am wondering what to prepare for George's Sunday meal.' The happy bride revealed that she will continue modelling, but will not be doing as much as she has been.

Opposite below: The newlyweds, with Brian Epstein behind. He shares the best man duties with Paul.

Left and above: Two weeks after their wedding, George and Pattie leave for Barbados. 'More of a holiday than a honeymoon,' says George.

What's it all about...

Paul and Jane Asher arriving at a private preview of her new film, *Alfie*. With them is Jane's brother Peter - of Peter and Gordon fame.

Opposite above: Not quite the fervour of a Beatles gig at the Italian Institue, Belgravia, as composer Luciano Berio introduces his latest work, *Un Omaggio a Dante* (A Homage To Dante). But the audience does include a famous fellow musician sitting attentively in the front row. The reason? Signor Berio specializes in electronic music, and Paul has indicated that the Beatles are experimenting with different sounds on their new album, *Revolver*.

Opposite below: Paul and Jane Asher arriving at the Plaza Cinema, Haymarket, London, for the première of *Alfie*.

Last British Concert

The Beatles give what is to be their last British concert, at Empire Pool, Wembley on 1 May. A British tour had been pencilled in for the end of the year, but this was eventually shelved, leaving the NME Poll Winners concert as the group's swan song for their home fans. It was a 15-minute, 5-song set: 'I Feel Fine', 'Nowhere Man', 'Day Tripper', 'If I Needed Someone' and 'I'm Down'. Although cameras were present, they stopped rolling for The Beatles' numbers because of a contractual dispute, so no footage exists of this milestone event.

Left: The Beatles rehearsing at BBC Television Centre for what was their only appearance on *Top of the Pops*. They perform the new single, 'Paperback Writer', and the B-side, 'Rain', which had been released six days earlier. Both songs had innovative features. As far as 'Paperback Writer' was concerned, it was neither a love song nor a dance number, and featured Paul playing what amounted to lead bass. On 'Rain' there was the distinctive sound of the backwards guitar. Some critics thought the group's bubble had burst, but the fans still made the single their tenth No 1 success.

The show is over...

Below: There is a delay in the flight which is to take the group to the United States for their final tour. To kill time they are shown round the new police station at London Airport.

The flight finally gets away, with the usual rousing accompaniment. The reception at the other end is less certain, as John's remarks on the relative popularity of The Beatles and Jesus are rehashed and misquoted. Bonfires are held to burn Beatles records and merchandise, before John eats a little humble pie and manages to smooth things over. In Canada, meanwhile, John has at least one ally in the shape of the Bishop of Montreal, the Rt Rev. Kenneth Maguire, who said: 'I wouldn't be surprised if The Beatles actually were more popular than Jesus. In the only popularity poll in Jesus's time he came out second best to Barabbas.'

But the show is over - the fans don't realize it yet, but John, Paul, George and Ringo knew this was the end of the line as far as touring and concert performance was concerned.

Not only ...But Also

The Beatles are in the middle of recording 'Strawberry Fields Forever', when John makes a guest appearance in a sketch for the Peter Cook and Dudley Moore Christmas show, *Not Only...But Also*. John plays the commissionaire of a 'members only' gents lavatory. The outside shots were filmed in Broadwick St, London W1.

Chapter Five

1967
Magical Mystery Tour

With no more touring to be done, The Beatles now needed to find a new focus for their lives. On the business front the group had formed The Beatles & Co, a legal partnership to handle all their business affairs that bound them together until 1977, but on a personal level each was looking in a different direction. George was already interested in India and its religions and music, and his passion for this grew and developed throughout the year. Ringo, who was always perhaps more home-loving than the others, began to spend extra time with his family. John tried acting, but decided he didn't like it or the company of most actors. Paul wrote some music for a film and tried a bit of painting.

Despite these different interests, they still wanted to be together to make music so they turned to the recording studio in earnest, working on their next LP, *Sgt Pepper's Lonely Hearts Club Band*. For some time they had all been experimenting with drugs, including LSD, which had a marked effect on their songwriting - in particular on John's work. The Lennon/McCartney partnership was now no longer really a partnership at all, as each was developing his skill in a different way; John was becoming rather introspective and wrote psychedelic and rather disorientating lyrics, while Paul's songs were much more bright and breezy.

The drugs also had another unexpected side-effect. Until now The Beatles public 'loveable mop-top' image had more or less survived against the odds, but 'A Day In The Life' from *Sgt Pepper* was the first Beatles song to be banned by the BBC, because of its supposed drug references. A couple of days later, when Paul admitted in the newspapers and on television that he had taken LSD, journalists jumped to condemn him. The band's stand on drugs was confirmed when all four Beatles, as well as Brian Epstein, signed a petition published in *The Times* calling for the legalization of marijuana. All this may have disgraced them in the eyes of parents and journalists, but to The Beatles' own generation it just added to their credibility.

But The Beatles themselves were still searching for the Meaning of Life and - having already decided that they were not the answer - had begun to give up drugs. It was at this point that they were introduced to the Maharishi Mahesh Yogi during his visit to London, by George's wife, Pattie. They all initially thought they had found what they were looking for, and threw themselves behind his movement. All four Beatles, as well as many other major pop stars, followed the Maharishi to Bangor in Wales to study transcendental meditation. The Press initially thought this was some sort of publicity stunt, but The Beatles soon made it clear that they were in earnest.

While they were in Wales, the news came of Brian Epstein's accidental death from an overdose of sleeping tablets. He was apparently rich, successful and happy, but behind the public façade he had felt increasingly lost and depressed after The Beatles gave up touring, since they no longer needed him as much. Despite their rather laid-back public response to the news, they were all devastated. John, in particular, felt that without a manager to lead and organize them, they were finished. At an emergency meeting held at Paul's house days after Brian's death, they discussed their future. Paul suggested they should try to cope by starting work on a project that had been postponed for some time: the filming of the *Magical Mystery Tour*.

The basis of this project was that they should all pile into a bus with a film crew and various other passengers, and just drive round England filming the adventures they were sure to have. There was no firm script, no experienced director and no one had any idea what they were doing. They spent a week driving round Cornwall, Devon and the South of England,

followed by photographers and journalists and causing chaos wherever they went, and a further week at West Malling Air Station – since no one had thought to book Shepperton Studios. The resulting ten hours of film, which took eleven weeks to edit down into the final one-hour version, was shown on BBC television at Christmas and was savagely criticized. The only good news was the music, six new songs written for the film that were also issued on a pair of EPs in a gatefold sleeve, with a 24-page booklet telling the story in photographs.

Perhaps the critics at the time did not make enough allowances for the experimental nature of the film, but by the time it was released The Beatles had moved on anyway. They now saw themselves as businessmen, building an empire in which they would be in total control. The first manifestation of this, the Apple Boutique, opened on Baker Street at the beginning of December.

Below: Paul greets Jane Asher at London Airport.
Previous page: At the photocall for the *Our World* TV broadcast, it is already evident from their different dress styles that each of The Beatles is developing as an individual.

1967: Chronology

6 January — The UK release of *The Family Way*, Paul's soundtrack LP of the music from the film

27 January — A new nine-year recording contract with EMI Records is signed by The Beatles

13 February — The single 'Strawberry Fields Forever'/'Penny Lane' is released in the US (17 February in the UK)

30 March — The famous cover photo for the *Sgt Pepper's Lonely Hearts Club Band* album is shot by Michael Cooper

19 April — A legal business partnership, The Beatles & Co, is formed to bind the group together until 1977

20 April — The first recording session for *Magical Mystery Tour* is held at EMI studios

15 May — While attending a performance by Georgie Fame at the Bag O' Nails Club in London, Paul meets photographer Linda Eastman

19 May — Brian Epstein holds a launch party for *Sgt Pepper's Lonely Hearts Club Band* at his home in London

20 May — The BBC imposes a radio and TV ban on 'A Day In The Life' because of the song's overt drug references

26 May — The LP *Sgt Pepper's Lonely Hearts Club Band* is released in the UK before the official date of 1 June (2 June in the US)

19 June — Paul admits on television that he has taken LSD

24 June — Photo-call and Press conference at Abbey Road studios for the *Our World* TV broadcast

25 June — The Beatles perform 'All You Need Is Love' on the world's first global satellite TV link-up, watched by 400,000,000. It is their last live TV performance

7 July — The single 'All You Need Is Love'/'Baby, You're A Rich Man' is released in the UK (17 July in the US)

24 July — John, Paul, George, Ringo and Brian Epstein lend their names to a petition that is published in *The Times*, calling for the legalization of marijuana

19 August — Ringo and Maureen have a second son, Jason

24 August — John, George and Paul, with wives and friends, attend a lecture by the Maharishi Mahesh Yogi at London's Hilton hotel and become interested in transcendental meditation

25 August — The Beatles and their entourage travel to Bangor, North Wales, to attend a weekend seminar by the Maharishi

27 August — Brian Epstein is found dead in bed at his London home

29 August — Brian Epstein's funeral is held in Liverpool. It is a family affair and is not attended by The Beatles

1 September — The Beatles all meet at Paul's house in St John's Wood to discuss their future

11 September — The Beatles set off in a coach with a camera crew and 43 passengers to begin shooting on their own TV film, *Magical Mystery Tour*

17 October — A memorial service is held for Brian Epstein at the New London Synagogue in Abbey Road

18 October — All The Beatles attend the première of *How I Won The War* at the London Pavilion

24 November — The single 'Hello,Goodbye'/'I Am The Walrus', is released in the UK (27 November in the US)

27 November — The LP *Magical Mystery Tour* is released in the US

3 December — Ringo flies to Rome to begin filming his part in *Candy*

5 December — John and George attend a party heralding the opening of The Beatles' Apple Boutique, two days later

8 December — The EP *Magical Mystery Tour* is released in the UK

25 December — Paul and Jane Asher announce their engagement

26 December — BBC1 transmits the première of *Magical Mystery Tour*

27 December — Paul appears live on *The David Frost Show* to defend *Magical Mystery Tour*

Here We Go Round The Mulberry Bush

Left: Paul and Jane Asher at the première of *Here We Go Round The Mulberry Bush*. Paul had been close to agreeing to write the music for the film, but eventually declined. Steve Winwood's Traffic got the job, and took the film's title song to No 8 in the charts.

Paul with his current car, an Aston Martin. It is during this period, the early part of '67, that he would later admit to experimenting with the 'heaven and hell' drug LSD.

Lonely Hearts Club Band...

Paul pictured at Heathrow after attending Jane Asher's 21st birthday party in Denver, Colorado. Stripes are in, but this is one Beatle moustache that's living on borrowed time.

Opposite: Paul meets Jane Asher at London Airport, following her five-month spell in the United States with the Bristol Old Vic. She would later remark how much changed she had found Paul on her return, citing the fact that she had not shared his experience with LSD.

Holiday time

Ringo heads off to Athens for a break with the Harrisons, wife Maureen remaining at home, heavily pregnant with their second child. It was around this time that The Beatles entered into serious negotiations to buy a Greek island haven for themselves, where they could escape the endless intrusions on their privacy. The group pull out of the deal at the last minute after Greek officials try to use it for publicity and propaganda purposes.

Paul and John return home from Greece.
Opposite: Paul with Jane Asher and four-year-old Julian Lennon.

Proud Dad

Ringo, with camera at the ready, arrives at Queen Charlotte's Hospital to visit Maureen and new baby son Jason, who was born the previous day.

Opposite above: Ringo and mother-in-law, Mrs Florence Cox. As Zak was named by Ringo, a fan of Western films, Maureen claims her turn by naming the new arrival - after the Greek mythological hero.

The Beatles become interested in transcendental meditation after attending a lecture by the Maharishi Mahesh Yogi in London (*opposite above*).

The Maharishi is going on to hold a conference in Wales, and all The Beatles decide to attend. Ironically, what is intended as a spiritual retreat turns into a scrum involving media and fans as news of the trip leaks out.

Paul at Euston Station, preparing to leave for
Bangor, North Wales, where the conference on
transcendental meditation is being held.

Below: John's £1000 floral make-over of his
Rolls-Royce causes quite a stir. The Phantom V
had been black, oozing Establishment, sobriety
and respectability. Six weeks at Fallon's
coachworks company, Chertsey, puts a stop to
all that.

Opposite: Paul at Newquay during the filming
of *Magical Mystery Tour*.

Taking them away - the Magical Mystery Tour

Above: No mystery here: the bus is simply too wide for the narrow Devon bridge and becomes well and truly stuck. It is an inauspicious start for the *Magical Mystery Tour*, Paul's pet project, conceived back in April, for a film with no form or script. It is September before shooting starts, a matter of days after Brian Epstein's death.

Opposite: On location in the West Country. Widecombe Fair and Newquay are among the stop-off points on the *Magical Mystery Tour*.

Left and overleaf: Paul and George pictured at the memorial service to Brian Epstein, held on 17 October at the New London Synagogue, Abbey Road.

How I Won The War

The day after Epstein's memorial service, Paul, George and Ringo, with partners and friends, attend the première of *How I Won The War* at the London Pavilion.

Below: John and Cynthia join the other Beatles for a front row view.

Ringo Sweet as Candy

Ringo looks to further his solo acting career by taking a minor part in the film *Candy*. Swedish beauty queen Ewa Aulin plays the nymphette of the title role.

Above: The director, Christian Marquand, shows Ringo how to look like a sex-mad Mexican gardener.

The Lennons and the Harrisons arriving at the Apple Boutique, Baker St, the first venture of their company which bears the same name.

Facing the music; Paul admits to mistakes, but does not regret making the film. The title should have informed people that there would be no plot or form, he says, adding: 'Was the film really so bad compared with the rest of the Christmas TV? Frankie and Bruce's (Messrs Howerd and Forsyth) show just wasn't funny, and you could hardly call the Queen's Speech a gasser.'

Chapter Six

1968

With A Little Help From My Friends

At the beginning of February, all four Beatles and their partners flew out to India to attend a three-month course in transcendental meditation at the Himalayan retreat of the Maharishi Mahesh Yogi. Ringo and Maureen had had enough after less than two weeks; the spicy vegetarian food did not agree with them and nor did the regime of chanting, meditation and mass praying. Paul and Jane stayed for only five weeks, but he claimed on his return that the trip had been a success and had done him good. The others left after nearly two months, when they heard rumours that the Maharishi had tried to enlighten some of the female members on the course in a physical rather than a spiritual way - although this later turned out to be just malicious gossip. George continued to pursue his interest in Indian culture and the Hindu religion, but the Maharishi was now out of the picture for good.

The Beatles turned their attention back to business, announcing the formation of Apple Corps Ltd. The plan was that Apple would have several divisions covering such areas as music, films, electronics, merchandise and the arts, and one of its functions was to provide creative people with funds to get them started – not in a philanthropic way, but as a business investment. It was a great idea in theory and Paul and John took it very seriously and went into the office regularly to direct operations. However, there was no one to organize everything on a proper business footing and to question if the funds going out would bring back any sort of return. The company soon became a source of easy money to every self-styled innovator, artist or hippy who happened to come through the door - and also to Apple executives and staff, who had lavish salaries, bought cars on their expense accounts and made the long lunch into an art form. It was to be some time before The Beatles realized what was happening and tried to take action.

Meanwhile a new Beatles film was ready for release: *Yellow Submarine*, a full-length animated feature film that had been two years in the making. It was based on one of The Beatles' earlier songs and they were consulted at the beginning, but they were not involved in working out the final concept or in developing the storyline. Even the voice-overs were spoken by actors, although the band did write a few new songs, as well as filming a short cameo appearance which was inserted near the end. The film did not do very good business in Britain because of poor distribution, but it went down very well in America and was highly regarded by the critics, often being referred to as 'the best film The Beatles never made'.

George returning from India. He had just completed
his first film score, composing and producing the
soundtrack for the film *Wonderwall*.

Opposite above: New four-piece band Grapefruit must
have hoped for even a fraction of the success of the
pop luminaries ranged behind them (*l to r:* Brian
Jones, Donovan, Ringo, John, Cilla Black, Paul). The
occasion was a Press reception at the Hanover Grand,
London, to mark the launch of the group's debut
single 'Dear Delilah'. The band, who had been
discovered by head of Apple Terry Doran, would make
little impact on the charts, however. 'Dear Delilah'
peaked at No 21, while their only other chart entry
was 'C'mon Marianne', which reached No 31.

Opposite below: John, Cynthia and George at the
Revolution Club, Mayfair, for a fashion show in which
Pattie takes to the catwalk. Next to John is Alexis
Mardas, otherwise known as Magic Alex, Apple's
electronics wizard.

Meditation

Paul's verdict on the Maharishi? 'Great feller...down-to-earth...no flashy cars.' Paul says that he and Jane both plan to meditate for an hour each day: 'Meditation is great. I'd recommend it to anyone'. In reality, The Beatles would all eventually conclude that the Maharishi offered no signpost along the road to spiritual enlightenment.

Returning five days later, each brandishing
the symbol of the newly-formed empire.
A client list that includes James Taylor and
Mary Hopkin - as well as The Beatles
themselves - ensures that Apple Records is
profitable from the beginning; other
branches of the corporation soon degenerate
into chaos and financial disaster.

Opposite: The Harrisons fly out to Nice.
Although the destination is France, George's
spiritual home is still India; his interest in
the religion, culture and music of the
country will endure.

Opposite below right and overleaf: Ringo and
Maureen en route to Cannes. Ringo reveals
that his diffidence about his own acting
talent led him to reject several starring roles
- including playing Dr Watson in a Sherlock
Holmes film - choosing instead the minor
part of the gardener in *Candy*.

In his Own Write

John and Yoko at the National Theatre for the first night of *In His Own Write*, a play adapted from two of Lennon's books and based loosely on his own childhood. With John and Yoko (*opposite below left*) is the play's co-producer, Victor Spinetti.

The Harrisons and Starrs returning from a trip to America, where George had taken part in the film *Raga*, with Ravi Shankar. In the same party is Cream guitarist Eric Clapton, one of George's best friends. When George and Pattie later drift apart, she will embark on an affair with Clapton and they subsequently marry. Clapton's song 'Layla' is believed to have been written with Pattie in mind.

Opposite and overleaf: Paul shows his musical eclecticism by turning his talents to the big brass sound. The occasion is the recording of a new McCartney composition, 'Thingumeybob', for the TV programme of the same name. It had originally been recorded in the studio, but Paul realized the sound wasn't quite right. Enter the Black Dyke Mills Band, Shipley, Yorkshire, for their moment of glory. Paul records both an indoor and outdoor version of the piece, and later says that the outdoor version will probably be used for the show, as it has a more authentic bandstand sound.

Back to his roots...

John goes back to his art college roots; he
holds an exhibition at the Robert Fraser Gallery,
Mayfair, consisting of a display of 50 charity
boxes. The exhibition is entitled *You Are Here*
and is dedicated to Japanese avant-garde artist
Yoko Ono.

And our friends are all aboard

It's like Beatlemania all over again as the group attend the London première of *Yellow Submarine*. Apart from the soundtrack, The Beatles' contribution to the film is minimal; they did not even select the song on which the animated feature would be based.

Opposite above left: Paul at his father's Wirral home, on the day after it is announced that his five-year-long relationship with Jane Asher is over.

Opposite: For once the hysteria is not generated by The Beatles in person. It is the closure of the Apple Boutique and the giving away of all the left-over stock that draws the massive crowds.

No more drugs

In October John and Yoko are charged with possession of cannabis at Marylebone Court and remanded on bail until 28 November.

John claims his drug-taking days are over as he is fined £150 for possession of cannabis. The charges against Yoko are dropped.

Opposite: Five-year-old Julian Lennon gets to see a circus with a difference: a rehearsal of *The Rolling Stones' Rock And Roll Circus*, featuring a host of stars performing circus and variety acts. John himself is down to do a spot of juggling, but the show never reaches the screen.

Chapter Seven

1969

All You Need Is Love

Their records were still outstandingly successful, but all four of The Beatles privately knew that as a group they were in trouble. Of them all, Paul was the most committed to keeping the band together and he also missed performing live in front of an audience. He reasoned that the main differences from the old days were that they no longer played together as a group and, because of spending weeks overlaying extra parts, took for ever to record each song. He decided that the solution lay in a return to performing live again and he tried to persuade the others to agree. Touring was definitely out, but they reluctantly decided to prepare for a concert or a television broadcast - with rehearsals being filmed for a documentary provisionally entitled *Get Back*, which was finally released as *Let It Be*.

The Beatles assembled at Twickenham Studios at the beginning of January, but almost immediately tensions within the group surfaced again, and this time it was George who walked out. He was persuaded to return, but the idea of doing a concert was shelved and they moved to their new Abbey Road recording studio to concentrate on making an LP. Keyboard player Billy Preston was invited to join them, which defused some of the tension and the recording proceeded. At the end of January, the group even played a live concert out of sight on the roof of the Apple building, which was filmed as part of

the documentary. However, the finished tapes for the LP itself sounded so bad that The Beatles decided not to release it for the moment and went back to the studio to start again. Perhaps everyone knew it was the end, but this time they were all on their best behaviour and the result was *Abbey Road*, one of their finest LPs.

At the beginning of 1969, the group had also realized that they needed to do something about Apple Corps Ltd, which had been losing money hand over fist ever since it was formed. However, they disagreed on who should be put in control to set matters straight. John and Yoko wanted Allen Klein, a tough New York businessman who was already involved in the music business, and they convinced George and Ringo to join them in appointing his company, ABKCO, to sort out Apple. But Paul didn't trust Klein and wanted instead the New York firm of Eastman & Eastman – run by his girlfriend Linda's father and brother. The others felt the Eastmans would just be looking out for Paul's best interests, so although they were appointed as general counsel it was under Klein. The band had never done anything before that was not unanimously agreed, but this time Paul was outvoted.

As well as Apple, there were other major problems in their business affairs that came to a head in 1969. The Beatles lost their controlling interest in Brian Epstein's old company, NEMS, and in Northern Songs, the company which published their songs. This meant that they no longer owned the rights to any

Let It Be

Filming the studio sessions for *Let It Be*.

Paul to marry?

Below: The rumour-mill is in overdrive concerning the last bachelor Beatle. Paul's name is linked with American photographer Linda Eastman, a 25-year-old divorcee with a six-year-old daughter.

Opposite: Linda Eastman takes flak from Paul's adoring female fans as the couple leave the Apple building in Paul's Mini. Paul has jettisoned the Castro-style beard which he sported for the celebrated Apple rooftop session a week earlier.

Right: The buck stops here. George declares an end to extravagant charitable giving. It follows a statement from John that they would all be broke in six months if the Apple Corporation continued haemorrhaging money at the present rate.

Paul and Linda at a launch party for Apple recording artist Mary Hopkin's debut album, held at the GPO Tower. The album had been produced by Paul (*opposite below*).

Opposite above: The couple attend the première of *Isadora* at the Odeon Theatre, St Martin's Lane.

It's official

On 11 March the rumours are proved to be true; Marylebone Register Office is booked for the following morning. Laid-back Paul buys the wedding ring which cost £12 'just before the shop shut'.

By Beatles' standards it is a quiet affair. There are no guests, and outside the register office photographers easily outnumber the assembled fans. Predictably, those who do turn up are mostly female and mostly distraught. Even so, Paul and Linda play safe and enter the building by a side door - past the dustbins (*above*).

At last...

Paul's best man is brother Mike McGear, of Scaffold fame, reversing their roles of the previous year, when Paul did the honours at Mike's wedding. Two hours after the register office ceremony, Paul and Linda have their marriage blessed by the Rev. Noel Perry-Gore, at St John's Wood Parish Church.

Surviving the crowds

Linda takes the opportunity to scotch Press reports that she is an heiress with family connections to Eastman-Kodak. 'I've been done, where's the money,' quips Paul.

George and Patti drugs charge

George and Patti are remanded on bail for cannabis possession at Esher and Walton Magistrates' Court (*below*), and are later fined £250 each on the drugs charge (*opposite*).

Right: Business as usual; the McCartneys have no immediate honeymoon plans and Paul gets straight back to work. He is seen here leaving Olympic Studios in London at 3.45 am after a recording session with Jackie Lomax on 13 March.

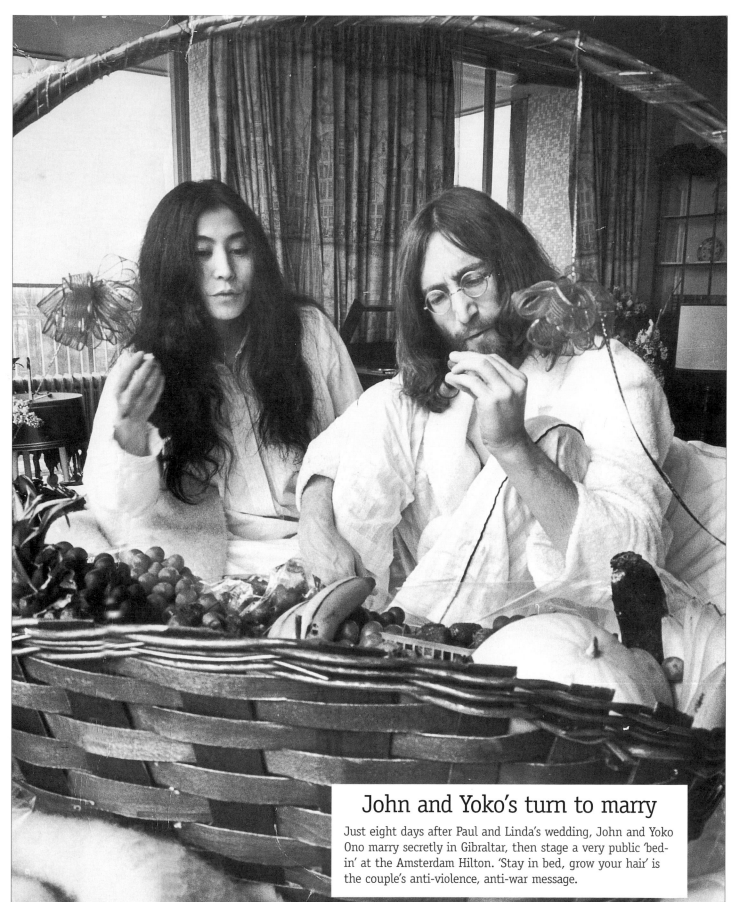

John and Yoko's turn to marry

Just eight days after Paul and Linda's wedding, John and Yoko Ono marry secretly in Gibraltar, then stage a very public 'bed-in' at the Amsterdam Hilton. 'Stay in bed, grow your hair' is the couple's anti-violence, anti-war message.

John and Yoko returning from Vienna on 1 April, where they saw the world première of *Rape*, their controversial production whose aim was to analyse the effect of blanket, intrusive TV coverage on an individual's life. In it, a girl is relentlessly pursued by a camera crew, who invade her life but refuse to speak to her. (*and overleaf*)

The Magic Christian

Ringo plays Peter Sellers' son in Terry Southern's satire *The Magic Christian*. The film's soundtrack features a McCartney song, 'Come And Get It', performed by Badfinger, a group signed to Apple.

Ringo and Peter Sellers throw their money around at a party celebrating the end of shooting. Each of the 300 guests invited to the Mayfair gaming club was given $1 million on arrival - but the faces on the notes bore an uncanny resemblance to Messrs Starr and Sellers and the money was valid only in the club casino.

The Ballad of John and Yoko

Five-year-old Kyoko Cox, Yoko's daughter by her previous marriage, flies in from New York on her own, to be met by her mother and famous new step-father. Meanwhile, Yoko makes her mark on the charts. The Beatles take 'The Ballad of John and Yoko' to No 1 in June; in the same month she and John record 'Give Peace A Chance', with a group of ad hoc musicians, The Plastic Ono Band. It reaches No 2.

Opposite left: Ringo makes sure his latest release gets into shot as he takes a break after the film is completed. Working on *The Magic Christian* had been a respite from the troubled Beatles' recording sessions, in which Ringo sometimes found himself sidelined, with Paul taking over on drums.

Opposite right: George returning from holiday in Sardinia. Like Ringo before him, George had actually quit The Beatles earlier in the year, following studio disagreements. Although he too returned a few days later, the cracks were now becoming impossible to paper over.

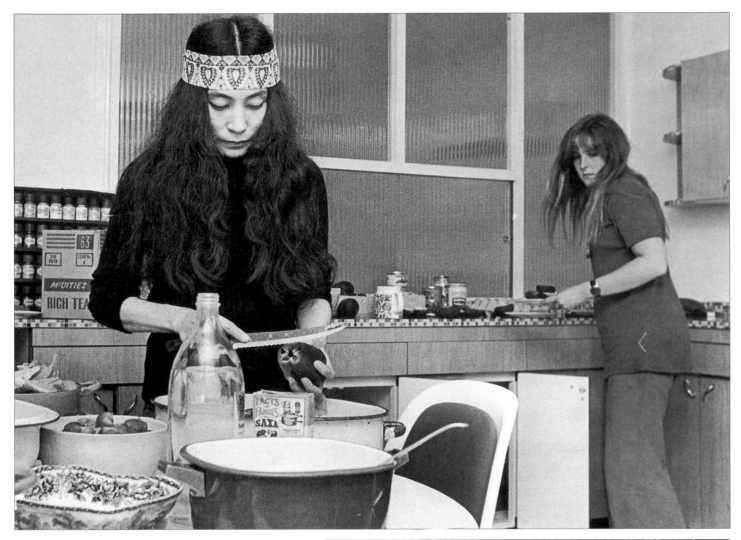

Kindred Spirits

George finds a group of kindred spirits at London's Radha Krishna Temple, a Hindu sect which trains people in the process of self-purification.

Opposite: Paul and Linda at the première of the film *Alfred The Great*.

Above: Yoko gets to grips with her new kitchen as she and John finally take up residence at Tittenhurst Park, a 60-acre estate with a mansion near Ascot. Cost: £145,000.

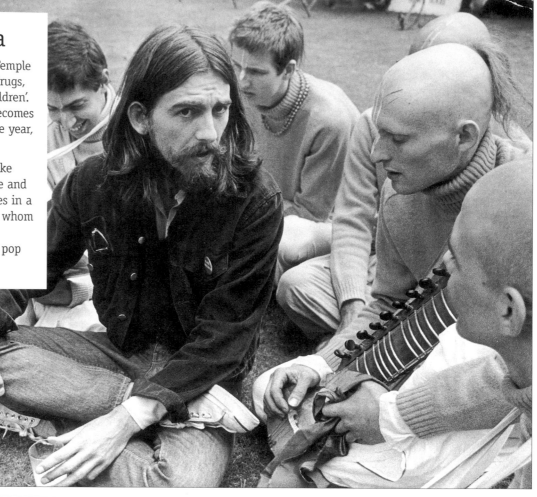

Hare Krishna

Members of Radha Krishna Temple shave their heads and ban drugs, alcohol and 'sex without children'. The 'Hare Krishna Mantra' becomes the unlikeliest pop hit of the year, peaking at No 12.

Opposite below: Just fans, like everybody else. John, George and Ringo, with spouses, are faces in a 150,000-strong crowd, all of whom have come to see Bob Dylan perform at the Isle of Wight pop festival in September.

From humble roots...

A far cry from 10 Admiral Grove where Ringo once lived in Liverpool, his new house in Kenwood (*opposite above*) has seven bedrooms, a heated swimming pool and nearly an acre of garden.

Opposite below: He also still owns a big house on the exclusive St George's Hill estate in Weybridge, which he bought in 1965, as well as a third home in Elstead.

James Hanratty

John and Yoko at a photo-call with
James Hanratty's parents, and fellow-
campaigner Edith Whicher.

The Lennons take up the case of
James Hanratty, the man hanged in
1962 for the murder of Michael
Gregsten in a lay-by on the A6 the
previous year. John and Yoko
announce that they plan to make a
film of the infamous case, the
anomalies in which played a part in
the abolition of the death penalty.

Below: A seven-o'clock shadow of his
former self. John's beard all but
disappears for a while - by all
accounts at Yoko's request.

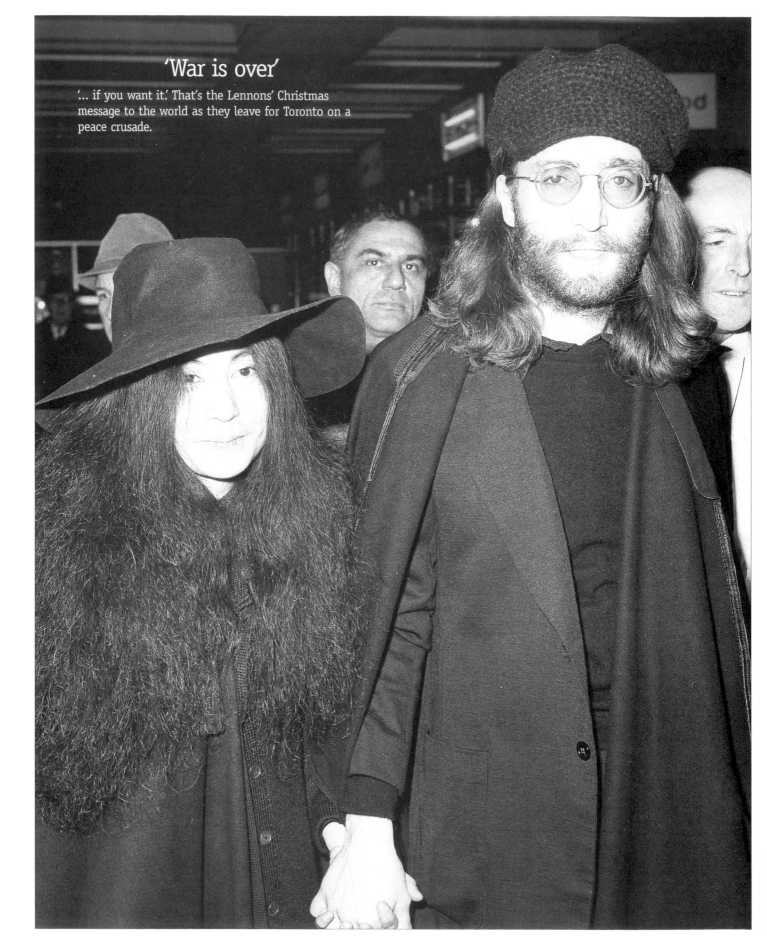

'War is over'

'... if you want it.' That's the Lennons' Christmas
message to the world as they leave for Toronto on a
peace crusade.

Chapter Eight

1970
Revolution

A t the beginning of 1970, John and Yoko hit the headlines again. An exhibition of John's lithographs at the London Arts Gallery was raided by the police and eight erotic pictures depicting him and Yoko on their honeymoon were confiscated. John had also been taking heroin regularly and early in the year he entered a clinic to be cured of his addiction. Ringo's film, *The Magic Christian*, had its première in New York in February and although the film did not do well, his performance was complimented. He also released his LP, *Sentimental Journey*, which was not well received by the critics but did briefly enter the American charts. George was working on his new LP, *All Things Must Pass* and Paul was putting the finishing touches to his first album, *McCartney*.

All The Beatles' contractual affairs were in a mess, and Allen Klein discovered that, despite what they had been led to believe, *Yellow Submarine* did not constitute the third in their three-film contract with United Artists. However, there had been enough material filmed for *Get Back*, their proposed television documentary, to turn it into a full-length feature film instead – which they could sell to UA. There was also the LP recorded at the same time, which had not been released due to its poor quality. None of The Beatles wanted to have anything more to do with this, so Allen Klein appointed

American producer Phil Spector to try and make something of it. His trademark was a dramatic, heavily orchestrated 'wall of sound' that had been used to great effect on other artistes' songs, but which was in total contrast to the way The Beatles normally recorded.

When the LP was ready for release, Paul was horrified to discover what had been done to it and in particular that his song 'The Long And Winding Road' had been almost swamped by the addition of a full orchestra and a female choir. He tried to insist that his original version was restored, but both Klein and the other Beatles ignored his protests. They also tried to delay the planned release of *McCartney*, so that it would not clash with the release of the Beatles LP and film, both now retitled *Let It Be* after one of Paul's songs. It was all too much, and in the press release that went out with advance copies of McCartney, Paul said that he had no plans to work with The Beatles again, and that he had not missed them while making his new LP. This was taken as an announcement that he was leaving The Beatles and the news prompted headlines in newspapers all round the world. The irony was that although Paul had been the first to say anything publicly, he was the last to make the decision that The Beatles were finished.

The film and LP *Let It Be* were released just afterwards, and the LP shot up the charts on a wave of nostalgia – even though most critics decided it was poor in quality and by no means showed The Beatles at their best. 'The Long And Winding Road'

All Things Must Pass

George renews his friendship with Ravi Shankar (*overleaf*) during an Indian Arts Season, held at the Royal Festival Hall in September. On the musical front, George enlists Phil Spector to produce his first solo project, the ambitious triple album *All Thing Must Pass*. They spend six months in the studio - compared to the six days Ringo spent making *Beaucoups of Blues*. It is well received by critics, and the record-breaking cover price does not deter the fans.

Opposite: Paul and Linda, looking serenely happy as The Beatles' split reverberates round the world.

Opposite: John and Yoko pictured in November, just prior to the release of the album *John Lennon/The Plastic Ono Band*, which reaches No 11 in the charts. It was around this time that Paul wrote to John on the subject of the dissolution of Apple. John replied with a postcard which read: 'Get well soon. Get the other signatures and I'll think about it.' It was responses such as these which precipitated Paul's decision to sue.

Below: George with Ravi Shankar.

Chapter Nine

1971

You Never Give Me Your Money

The High Court case to dissolve The Beatles' company was heard in London during February and March and Paul was the only Beatle to attend, supported by his wife, Linda. The others still believed that Allen Klein was their saviour so they felt that Paul was merely out to cause trouble. At the time he was also disliked by many fans and was having a hard time in the Press because they all blamed him for breaking up the group. He claimed he was not going through the court case just for himself, but for all the Beatles, since their entire empire was about to vanish into someone else's pocket. His counsel pointed out that Paul would actually be better off sticking to the terms of the original agreement, since the most successful record of that financial year had been George's single, 'My Sweet Lord', which had become the best-selling single of 1971. However, it soon became apparent that Allen Klein had taken at least $500,000 more than he was entitled to on The Beatles' American royalty deal, and the High Court judge finally ruled in favour of Paul. The other three Beatles were furious, but at the same time felt a sense of release - now they were really free to pursue individual careers.

George was initially riding high, with both his last LP and his latest single at the top of the charts. Unfortunately an American music publisher then claimed that 'My Sweet Lord' plagiarized a hit of the 1960s, 'He's So Fine', by the Chiffons. The court battles were to go on for years, before George was defeated and had to pay out thousands of dollars. Meanwhile his interest in India led him to organize *Concert For Bangladesh*, two concerts at Madison Square Garden in New York in aid of famine victims. The first was of Indian music specially composed by Ravi Shankar and the second boasted an all-star line-up, all performing for free, including George, Ringo, Bob Dylan and Eric Clapton. The concerts, with an accompanying album and film, raised an enormous amount, well over $10m. Unfortunately a great deal of money was creamed off by the various record companies involved and by the tax authorities - even though all the proceeds were for charity - and only a small percentage of the total actually made it to Bangladesh.

John released one of his most critically acclaimed solo albums, *Imagine*, which topped the charts in both Britain and America. The songs were much more gentle - more commercial and less avant-garde - than those John had released previously, but also included a bitter attack on Paul in a song called 'How Do You Sleep?'. This was also the year that John was allowed back to America. For several years he had been refused entry because of his drug convictions, but in September 1971 the authorities relented and John and Yoko flew to New York for a short visit, which turned into a permanent stay. The Press in Britain had done nothing but ridicule them and their beliefs and make fun of Yoko as an

It's easy if you try...

With the release of *Imagine* still several weeks away, Yoko takes centre stage with the publication of her book *Grapefruit*. Yoko had published 500 copies of her collection of 'instructional poems' some seven years earlier, and had sent John a copy. The content was a series of enigmatic thoughts, such as: 'Draw a map to get lost' and 'Smoke everything you can, including your pubic hair.'

Opposite: Paul and Linda host a gala evening at the Empire Ballroom, Leicester Square, to launch their new group, Wings.

Fledgling group

Drummer Denny Siewell (*left*) and Denny Laine, the ex-Moody Blues
guitarist/vocalist complete the Wings line-up.

That'll Be The Day

Ringo looked great in *That'll Be the Day* (*below right*), which was set in the late 1950s. It was almost a recreation of his youth, since his character was based in a summer holiday camp similar to the Butlin's camps he had worked in with Rory Storm and the Hurricanes before he joined The Beatles.

After filming had finished Ringo began work on his new LP, *Ringo*, but although things were going well professionally, personally he and Maureen were on the verge of splitting up.

Opposite above left: Paul and Linda during Wings' UK tour.

Opposite below left: 'That's my daddy' - Stella joins Paul and Linda at a photo-call.

Opposite above right: Even in the Seventies, Paul and Linda were involved in charitable causes. In November 1973 they made a surprise visit to the Toy For a Sick Child Fund in Piccadilly, where two-year-old Stella donated her teddy, Fruity.

Opposite below right: John in Los Angeles, during his separation from Yoko.

On your bike...

Now that all the legal problems of The Beatles break-up were far behind him, Paul seemed more relaxed. He developed a reputation as a family man, spending his free time with Linda and the children.

Below: The McCartneys on the move again, this time off to New Orleans where Paul was recording for his new LP, *Venus and Mars*. Paul had recently met up with John and George in New York, so the Press was full of rumours about The Beatles reforming.

Wings over water...

Below right: Paul chats to George Harrison during a party for Wings, which was held by Capitol Records aboard the liner *Queen Mary* at Long Beach.

Right: George was going through a bad time during this period. His marriage to Pattie had hit the rocks, and his last LP, *Dark Horse*, had quickly been dubbed 'Dark Hoarse' by the critics because of the poor state of his voice.

Below and opposite below: Another tour for Wings, this time their first, and only, tour round the world. The first section began with concerts all round Britain, after which they moved on to Australia.

Opposite above: Linda relaxes during the tour, while Paul entertains Stella and her playmate, Tamsy Lee.

Wings at Wembley

Opposite: Wings give two concerts at the Empire Pool, Wembley, playing to 8,000 people. Two 'journalists' from the USSR also attended one of the concerts, and Paul announces that he hopes to tour Russia in the near future.

After his split from Maureen, Ringo was seen around the world with several different women, including Nancy Andrews and Shelley Duvall. At one point he even became engaged to Nancy, but it was short-lived.

Out on the town...

Right: Paul attends the première of *Billy*.

Below right: At the wedding reception for Mike Leander, Gary Glitter's manager, and Penelope Carter at the Ritz Hotel, Piccadilly.

Opposite above: Susan George and Marc Bolan join Paul and Linda at a backstage party at Olympia to celebrate Rod Stewart's comeback concert in 1976. Rod himself missed the party – he went home early to shake off a heavy cold.

Opposite below: Although they were expecting to have another girl, Paul and Linda's first son, James Louis, made his appearance on 12 September 1977. Linda took the first picture of him herself using a timing device, and was photographed doing so by the *Daily Mail*'s Press Photographer of the Year, Monty Fresco.

Eight days in jail...

Paul faces the Press at the gates of his Sussex farm, fresh from eight days in prison and deportation from Japan after a large stash of cannabis was found in his luggage. But things soon begin to look up when he receives two more music industry awards: Paul with Linda (*opposite below left*) arriving at the Café Royal to receive the Outstanding Music Personality at the British Rock and Pop Music Awards; later in the year, Yul Brynner (*opposite below right*) presents Paul with a Special Ivor Novello Award for his services to British music, at a West End celebrity lunch.

Opposite above left: Paul, still popular with all ages, is mobbed by fans wanting his autograph.

Opposite above right: Although becoming obsessive about his privacy, George is busy launching his company, HandMade Films, which involves travelling between London and the film capital of the world, Los Angeles.

A celebration party at the Hippodrome night-club (*below right and opposite above left*), before the London première of *Give My Regards to Broad Street* at the Odeon, Leicester Square, is attended by Paul, Linda, Ringo and Barbara and Olivia Harrison. George can't make the première, because he is in New Zealand attending a literary luncheon to help Derek Taylor – once Brian Epstein's assistant and then The Beatles' Press Officer during their Beatlemania days - promote his new book, *Fifty Years Adrift*.

Opposite below: Ringo, always ready for a party, dresses in gold brocade for a Chelsea Arts Club masked ball with a Venetian carnival theme. Barbara wears an equally extravagant costume with a head-dress of gold roses.

Opposite above right: Ringo becomes the first grandfather Beatle when his daughter-in-law, Sarah Starkey, gives birth to a girl, Tatia Jane.

It was 20 years ago today...

Opposite: At a massive party to celebrate the 20th anniversary of the official release date of *Sgt Pepper's Lonely Hearts Club Band*, Paul cuts a slice of cake, helped by Linda and artist Peter Blake, who created the cover picture.

Back on stage again for the Prince's Trust Rock Concert in June '87, George's guests include Ringo, Eric Clapton, Elton John and Phil Collins.

On the road again

Paul still loved performing in public, and at the end of the Eighties he formed a new band to back him during a twelve-month world tour beginning in July 1989. The line-up included Linda as usual, with guitarists Hamish Stuart and Robbie McIntosh, drummer Chris Whitten and keyboard player Wix. On tour Paul is the star, with the others merely a backing band. Refusing any sponsorship, Paul dedicated the tour to Friends of the Earth - which didn't mean that they received any profits but did give them a platform for their views in the programme.

Opposite below right: Paul finishes the Eighties with yet another award, a miniature gold copy of his own guitar, presented by the Performing Right Society for his contribution to pop music. At the lunch held at Claridge's Paul is given a standing ovation by guests, who included violinist Nigel Kennedy, Bee Gees Maurice and Robin Gibb, Bruce Welch from The Shadows, Chris Rea and song-writer Tim Rice.

Simply the best

When *Q* magazine published its 100 Greatest Stars of the Twentieth Century, based on readers' votes, John Lennon was No 1, Paul was next at No 2, Ringo came in at No 26 and George at No 36.

Opposite top right: Sir Paul McCartney arrives at the Ivor Novello Awards at the Grosvenor House hotel.

Opposite top left: In July 2001, Paul became engaged to former model Heather Mills, whom he met through her charity work. They became engaged during a short break in the Lake District where Paul presented Heather with a sapphire and diamond engagement ring which he bought on a trip to India.

Opposite bottom: Paul and his daughter Mary at the Chloé show by Stella McCartney, Paris Fashions, Pret-a-Porter.

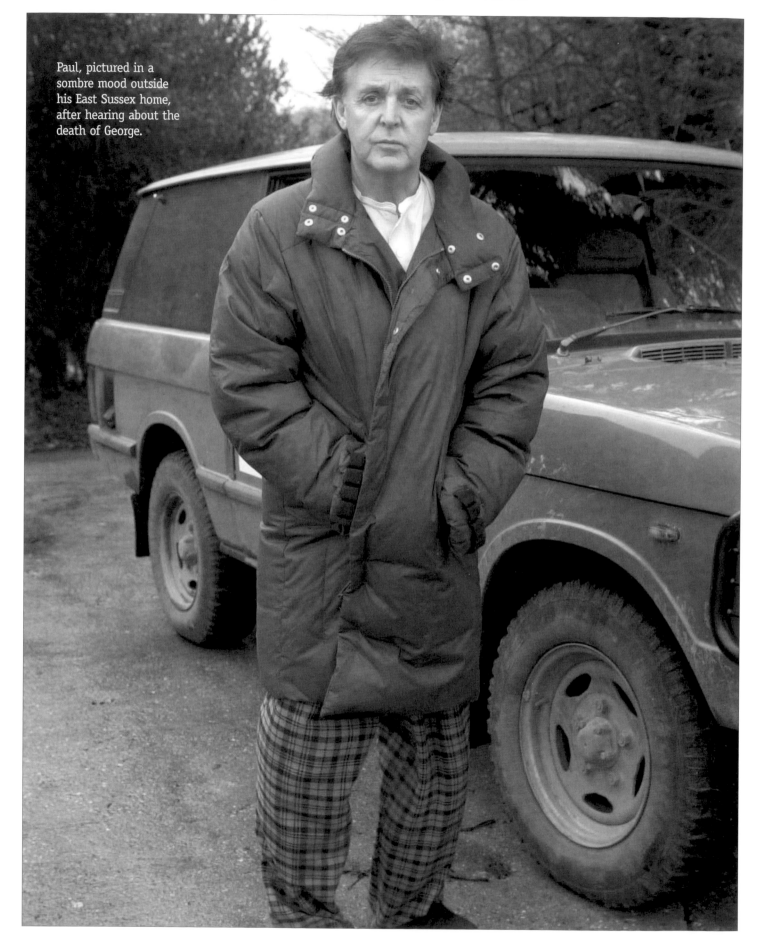

Paul, pictured in a sombre mood outside his East Sussex home, after hearing about the death of George.

1972-2002: Chronology

1972

8 Jan — The triple LP of George's Bangladesh benefit concert, *The Concert For Bangla Desh*, is released in the UK (20 February in the US)

9 Feb — Wings start an impromptu tour of British universities by appearing unannounced at Nottingham University

25 Feb — Paul releases another single, 'Give Ireland Back To The Irish'/'Give Ireland Back To The Irish (version)' in the UK (28 February in the US)

28 Feb — George and Pattie are injured in a minor car accident in Maidenhead

17 Mar — Ringo releases his second single 'Back Off Boogaloo'/'Blindman' in the UK (20 March in the US)

18 Mar — At the Empire Pool, Wembley, Ringo directs the filming of T. Rex in concert for the Apple film, *Born to Boogie*

May — The film of *The Concert For Bangladesh* is shown at the Cannes Film Festival, after its world première in New York on 23 March

12 May — Wings release their first single, 'Mary Had A Little Lamb'/'Little Woman Love' in the UK (29 May in the US)

21 May — BBC Radio One begins a serial, *The Beatles Story*

5 Jun — George and Ravi Shankar are given an award by UNICEF in recognition of their efforts in aid of refugees in Bangladesh

12 Jun — John and Yoko release their double LP, *Some Time In New York City* in the US (15 September in the UK)

9 Jul — Wings begin a European tour with a concert at Châteauvallon in France

10 Aug — Paul and Linda are charged with possessing drugs in Sweden

30 Aug — John and Yoko stage two charity concerts at Madison Square Garden in New York in aid of handicapped children

20 Sept — Scottish police raid the McCartneys' farm and find cannabis plants

16 Oct — Shooting of Ringo's new film, *That'll Be the Day*, begins in the UK

1 Dec — Paul releases another single, 'Hi Hi Hi'/'C Moon' in the UK (4 December in the US)

14 Dec — Ringo attends the world première of *Born to Boogie* in London

23 Dec — The world première of John and Yoko's film, *Imagine*, on US television

1973

9 Mar — Paul is fined £100 for growing five cannabis plants

18 Mar — Wings play a benefit for Release at London's Hard Rock Café

23 Mar — The first single from Paul and Wings, 'My Love'/'The Mess' is released in the UK (9 April in the US)

31 Mar — Allen Klein and ABKCO reach the end of their term as business managers of Apple and other Beatles companies

2 Apr — A pair of double LPs are released in the UK, *The Beatles 1962-1966* and *The Beatles 1967-1970* (19 April in the US)

12 Apr — The world première of *That'll Be the Day* at the ABC cinema in Shaftesbury Avenue is attended by Ringo, Maureen, Paul and Linda

16 Apr — Paul's TV film, *James Paul McCartney*, is shown on US television (10 May in the UK)

30 Ap — Paul and Wings release an LP, *Red Rose Speedway*, in the US (4 May in the UK)

11 May — Wings begin their first proper tour of the UK with a concert in Bristol

26 May — George releases a single, 'Give Me Love (Give Me Peace On Earth)'/'Miss O'Dell', in the UK (7 May in the US)

30 May — George releases another LP, *Living In The Material World* in the US (22 June in the UK)

1 Jun — Paul releases a single of the James Bond theme that he has written, 'Live And Let Die'/'I Lie Around'

4 Jul — Wings start another short tour of the UK with a concert in Sheffield

5 Jul — The world première of *Live and Let Die* at the Odeon, Leicester Square, attended by all of Wings

24 Sept — Ringo releases his single, 'Photograph'/'Down And Out' in the US (19 October in the UK)

Oct — John separates from Yoko and flies to Los Angeles with their secretary, May Pang

26 Oct — Paul releases 'Helen Wheels'/'Country Dreamer' in the UK (12 November in the US)

2 Nov — John, George and Ringo sue Allen Klein for misrepresentation in the High Court, and Klein counter-sues

2 Nov — John releases the LP, *Mind Games* and the single, 'Mind Games'/'Meat City' in the US (16 November 1973 in the UK)

2 Nov — Ringo releases his LP, *Ringo*, in the US (23 November in the UK)

3 Dec — Another single from Ringo, 'You're Sixteen'/'Devil Woman' is released in the US (8 February 1974 in the UK)

5 Dec — Paul and Wings release *Band On The Run* in the US (7 December in the UK)

1974

15 Feb — Release in the UK of the Paul and Wings single, 'Jet'/'Let Me Roll It', from *Band On The Run* (18 February in the US)

18 Feb — Ringo releases his single, 'Oh My My'/'Step Lightly' in the US. In the UK the B side is 'No No Song' and the single is released 9 January 1976

8 Apr — Release in the US only of the Paul and Wings single 'Band on the Run'/'Nineteen Hundred and Eighty Five'

28 Jun — Release in the UK only of the Paul and Wings single, 'Band On The Run'/'Zoo Gang', from *Band On The Run*

23 Sept — John releases his single, 'Whatever Gets You Through The Night'/'Beef Jerky', in the US (4 October in the UK)

26 Sept — John releases his LP, *Walls And Bridges* in the US (4 October in the UK)

18 Oct — UK release of 'Walking in the Park with Eloise'/'Bridge Over the River Suite', by the Country Hams, a pseudonym for Paul and Wings with Floyd Cramer and Chet Atkins (2 December in the US)

25 Oct — Paul releases his single, 'Junior's Farm'/'Sally G' in the UK (4 November in the US)

28 Oct — Allen Klein loses his court case against John, George and Ringo

2 Nov — George begins his solo tour of the US with a concert at the Pacific Coliseum, Vancouver

11 Nov — Ringo releases his single, 'Only You'/'Call Me' in the US (15 November in the UK)

15 Nov — Ringo releases his LP, *Goodnight Vienna* in the UK (18 November in the US)

16 Nov — John has his first solo No 1 in the US, when 'Whatever Gets You Through The Night' reaches the top of the *Billboard* chart

18 Nov — George releases his single, 'Dark Horse'/'I Don't Care Anymore' in the US only. In the UK the B side is 'Hari's on Tour (Express)' and the single is released on 28 February 1975

6 Dec — George releases his single, 'Ding Dong'/'I Don't Care Anymore' in the UK only

9 Dec — George releases his LP, *Dark Horse* in the US (20 December in the UK)

16 Dec — First US release of John's single, '#9 Dream'/'What You Got' (31 January 1975 in the UK)

1975

Jan — John returns to Yoko in New York

9 Jan — The Beatles & Co partnership is formally dissolved in the London High Court

16 Jan — Wings begin to record for their next album, *Venus and Mars*

27 Jan — Release in the US only of Ringo's single 'No No Song'/'Snookeroo'

7 Feb — Paul and Wings' single, 'Junior's Farm'/'Sally G' is re-issued in the UK only, with the A and B sides swopped round

17 Feb — John releases his LP, *Rock 'n' Roll* in the US (21 February in the UK)

21 Feb — Release in the UK only of Ringo's single 'Snookeroo'/'Oo Wee'

1 Mar — John and Yoko appear together again in public, at the Grammy Awards in the US, where John is a guest presenter

3 Mar — Linda is arrested and charged in the US with possession of cannabis

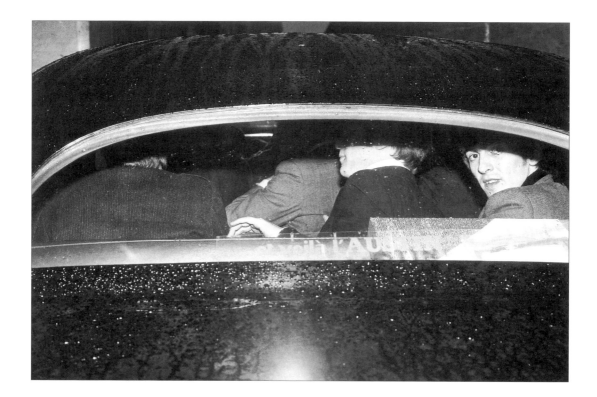

Bibliography

The Beatles – Hunter Davies (London, Arrow Books, 1992)

The Beatles: 25 Years in the Life, A Chronology 1962-1987 – Mark Lewisohn (London, Sidgwick & Jackson, 1987)

The Beatles Files – Andy Davis (UK, Colour Library Direct, 1998)

The Complete Beatles Chronicle – Mark Lewisohn (London, Hamlyn, 1992)

The Complete Idiot's Guide to The Beatles – Richard Buskin (New York, Alpha Books, 1998)

The Love You Make – Peter Brown & Steven Gaines (London, Macmillan, 1983)